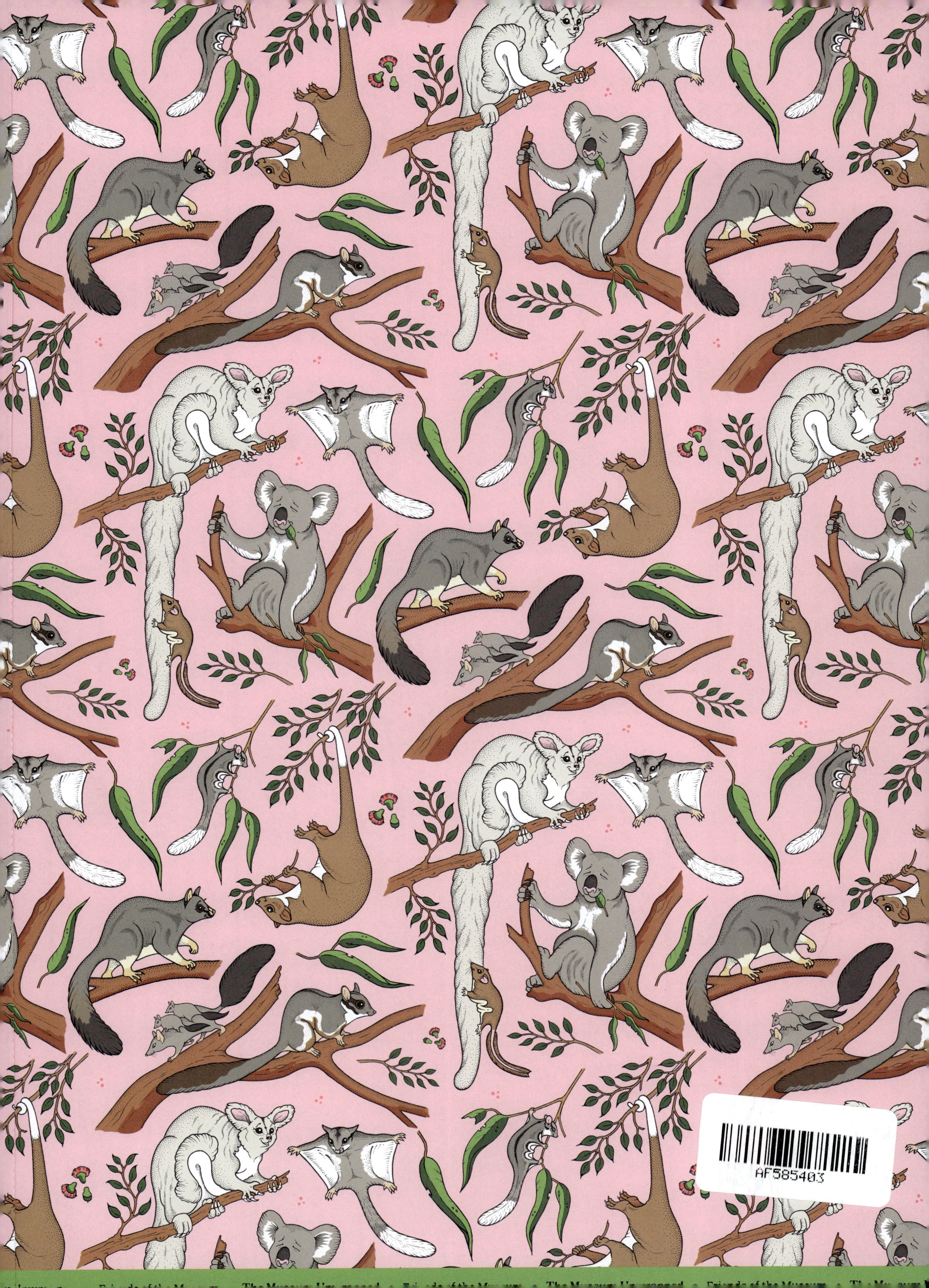
AF585403

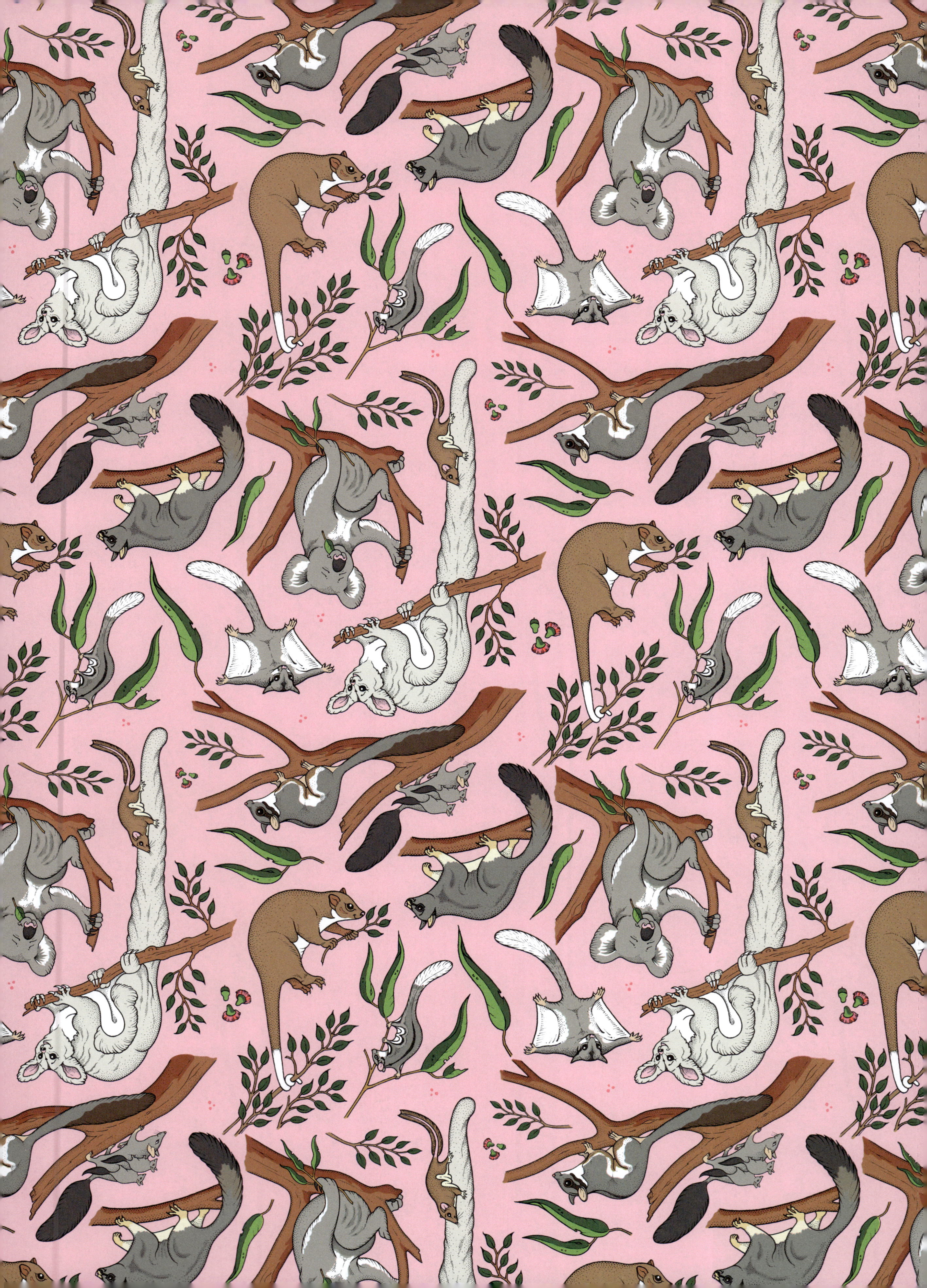

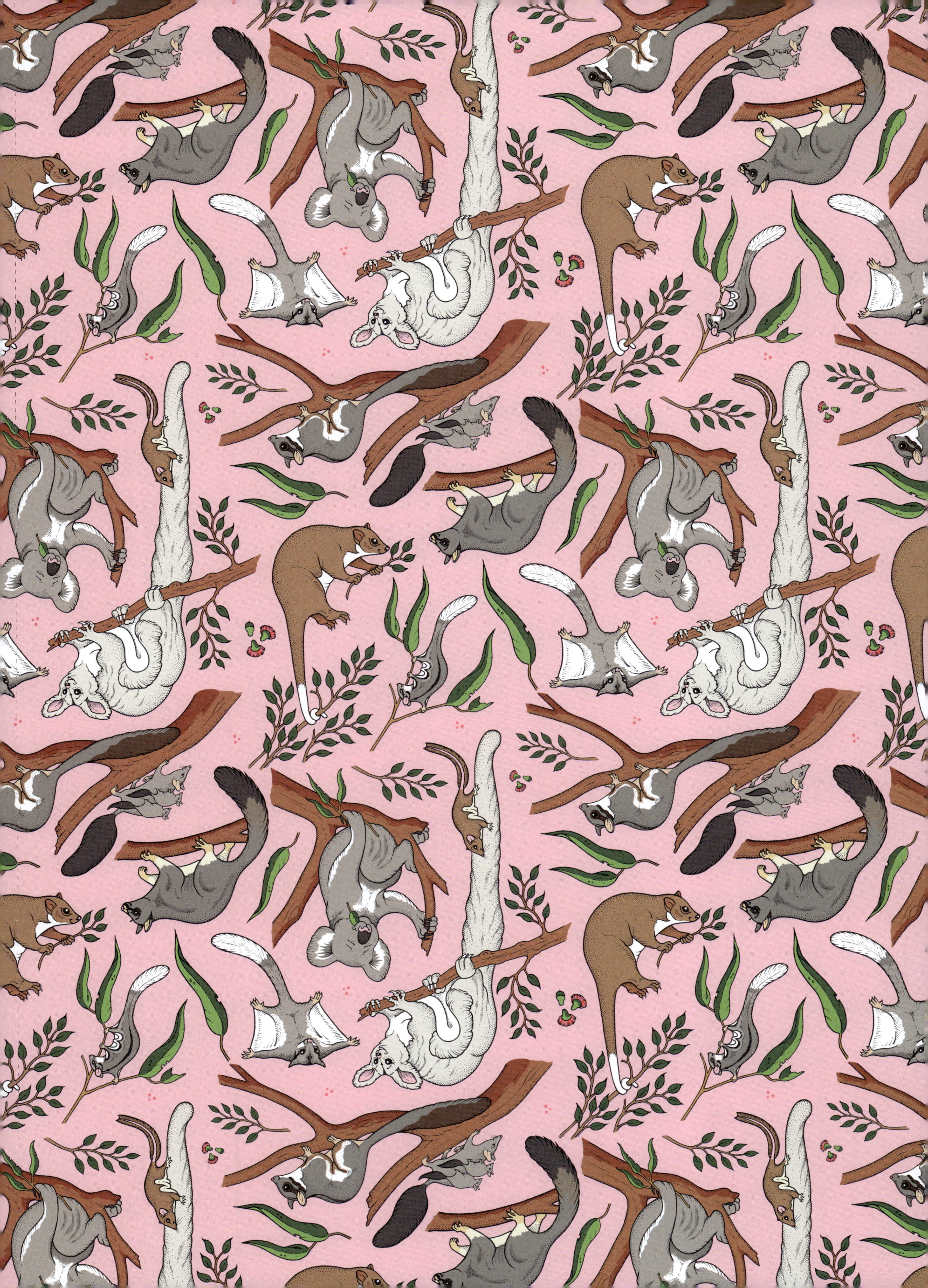

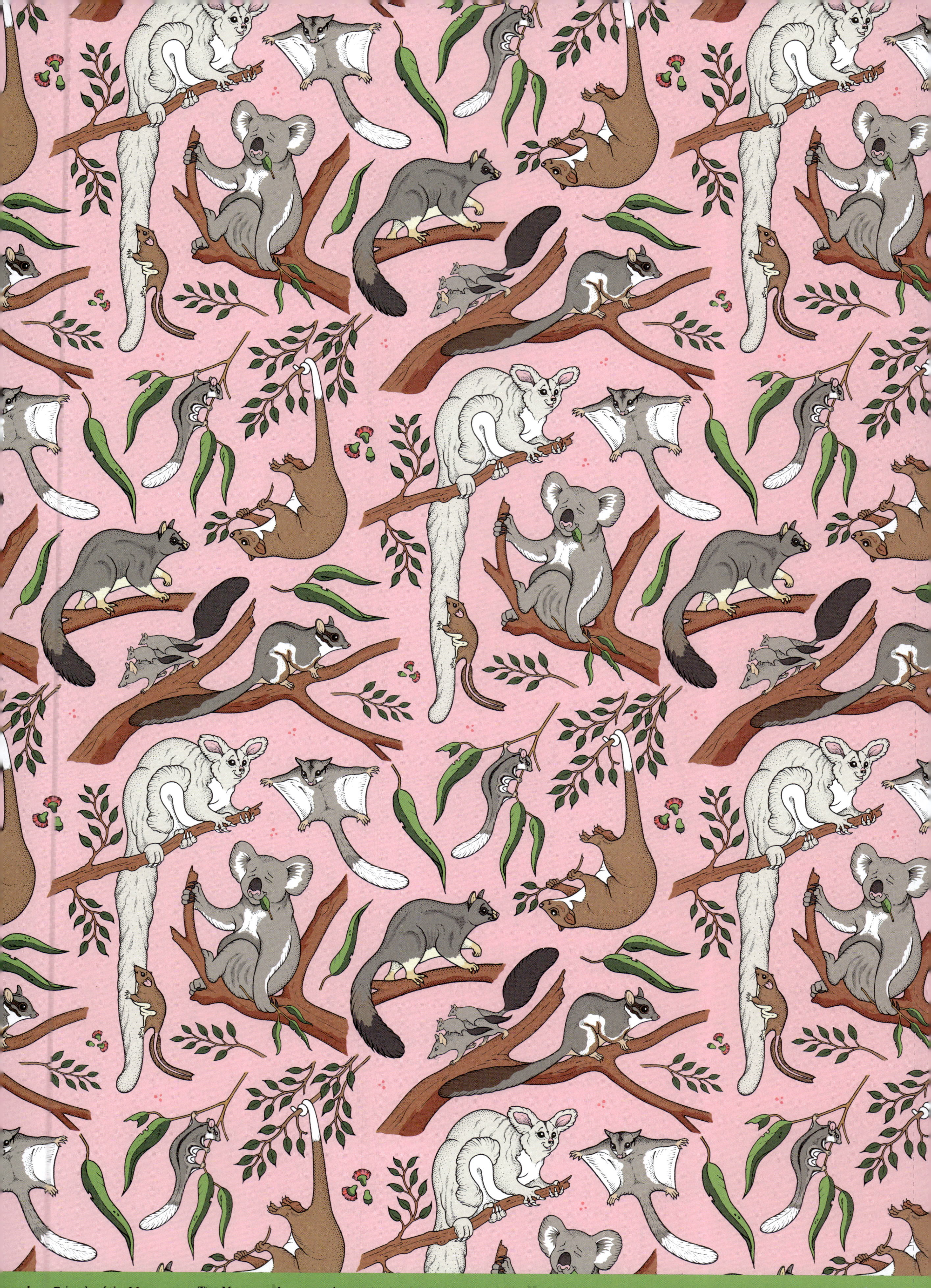

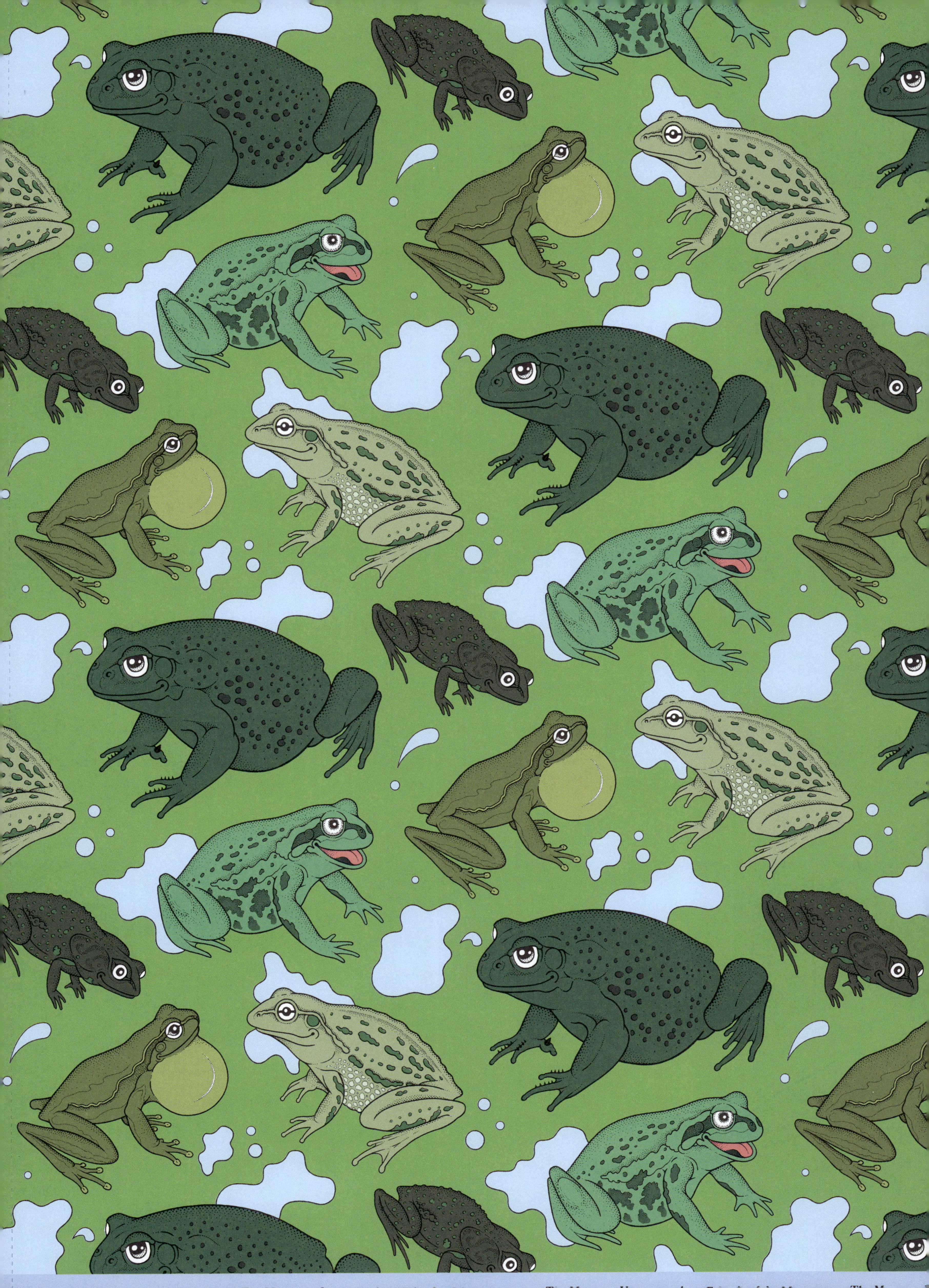

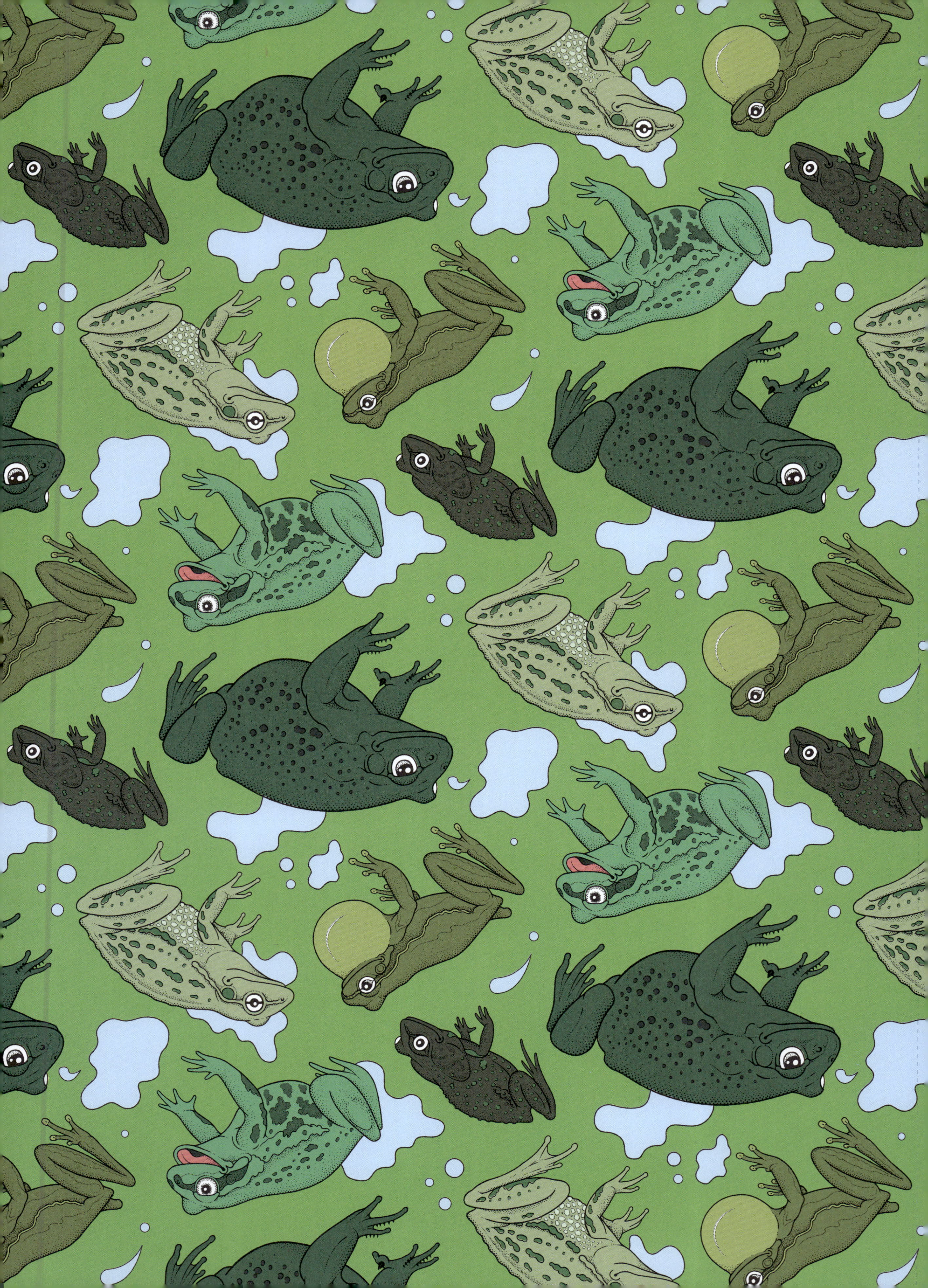

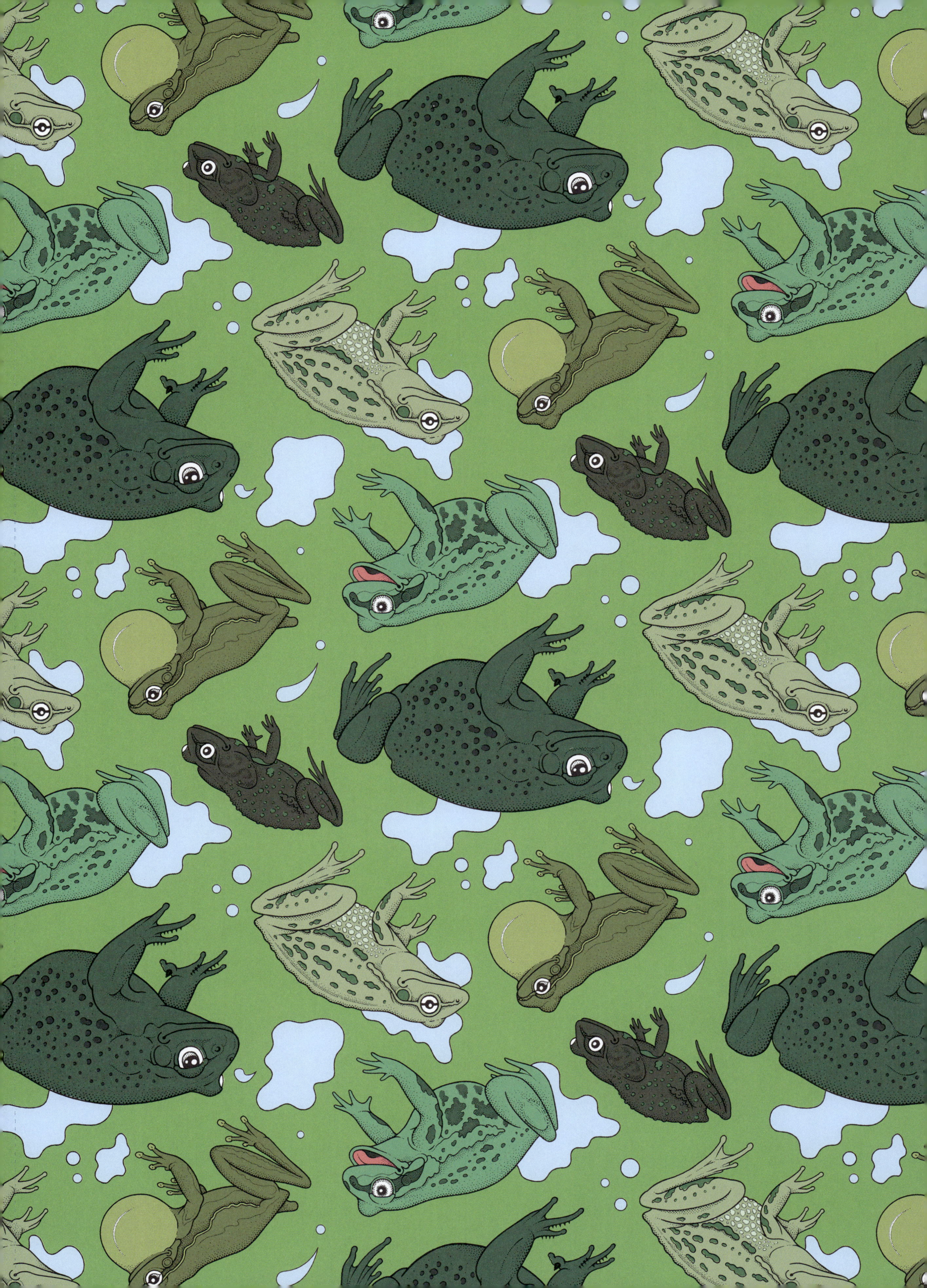

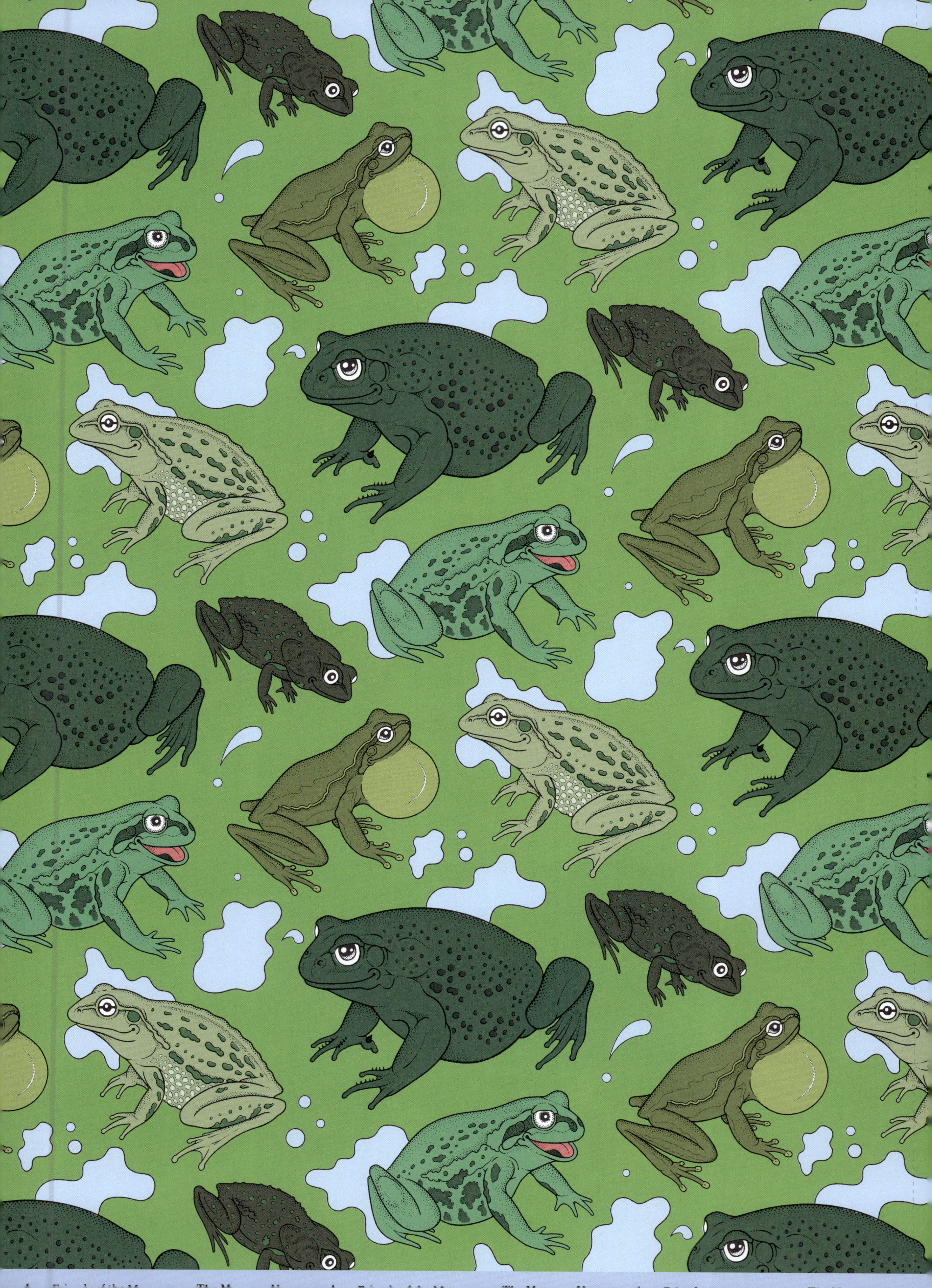

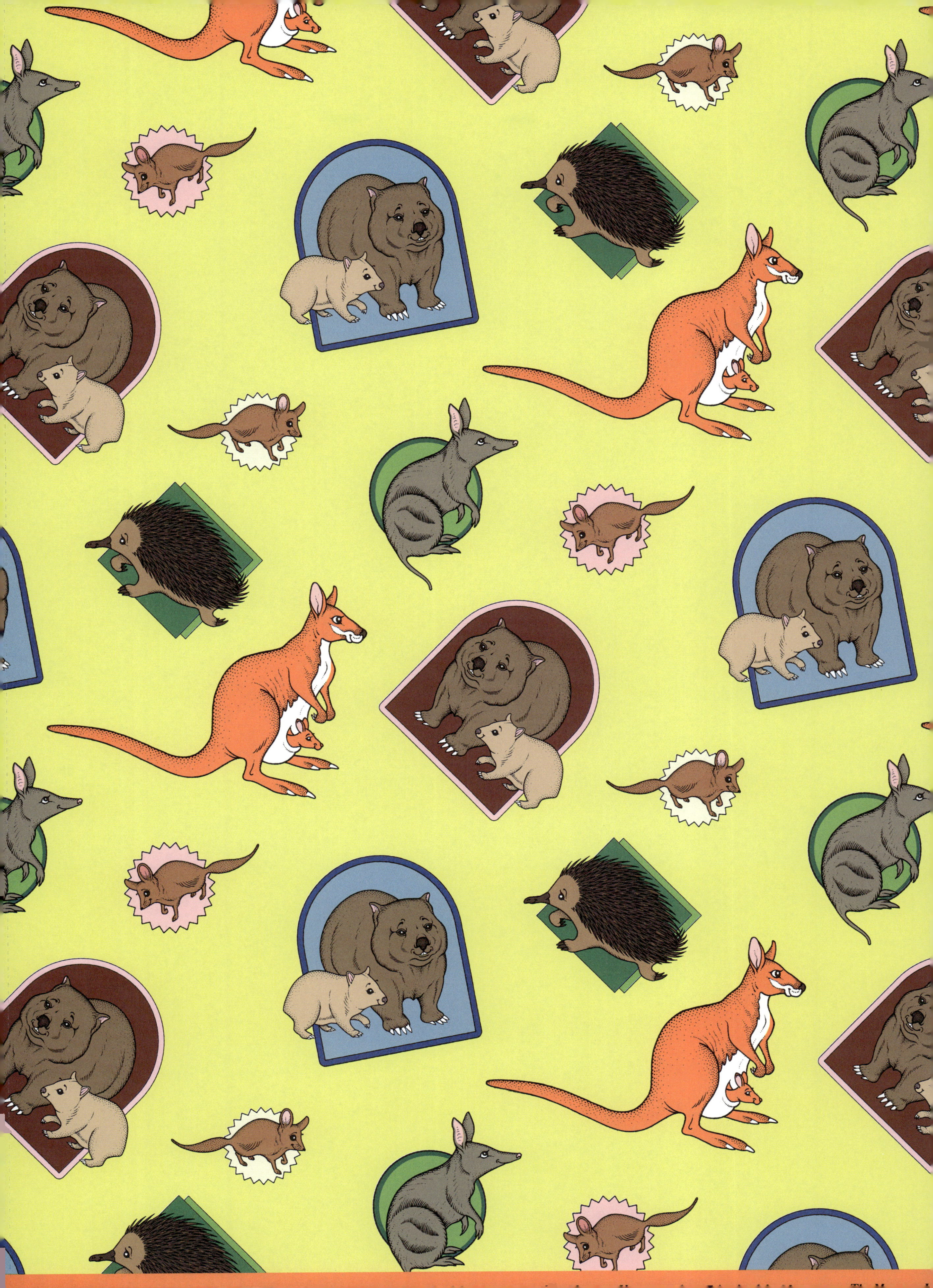

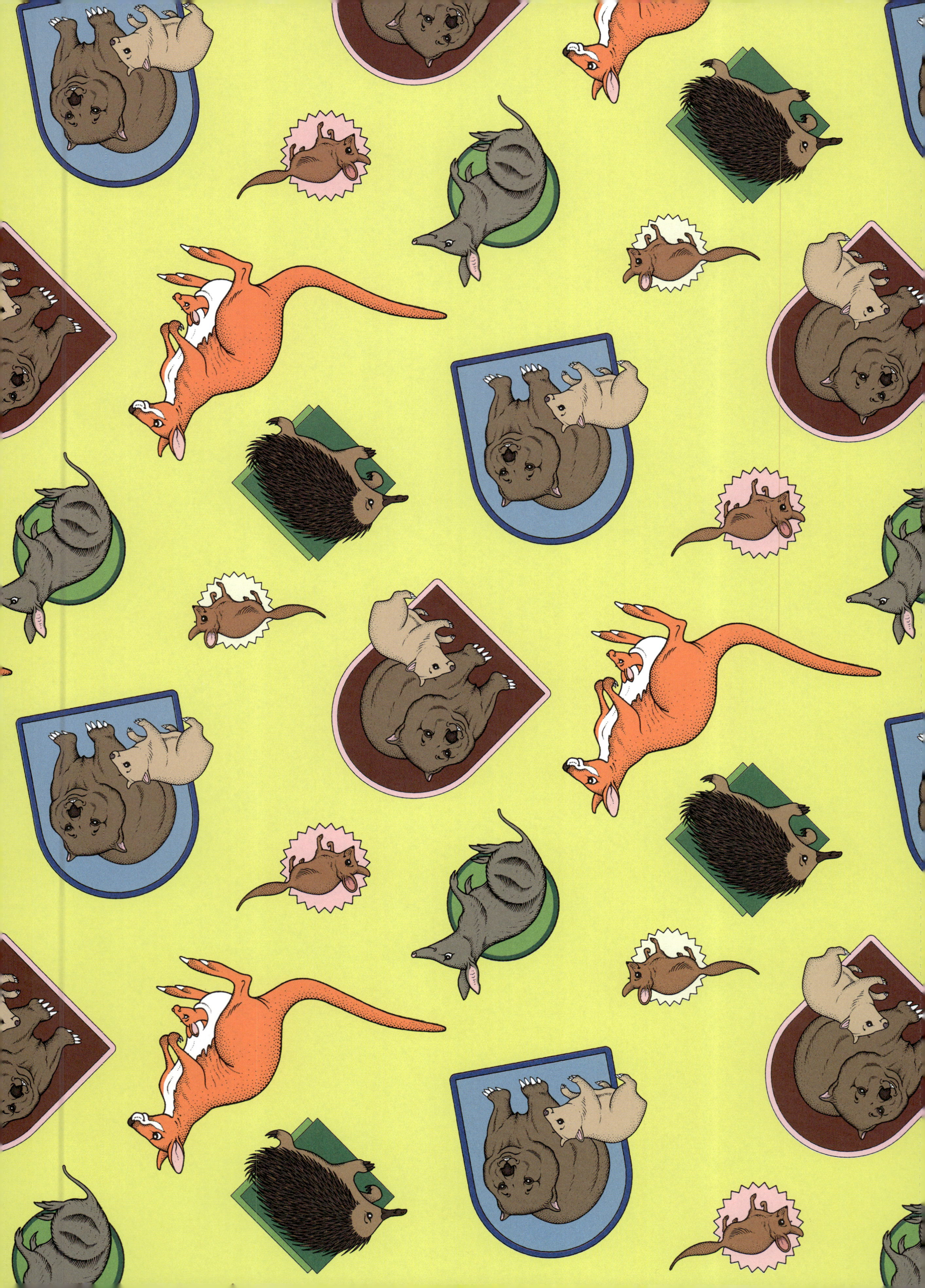

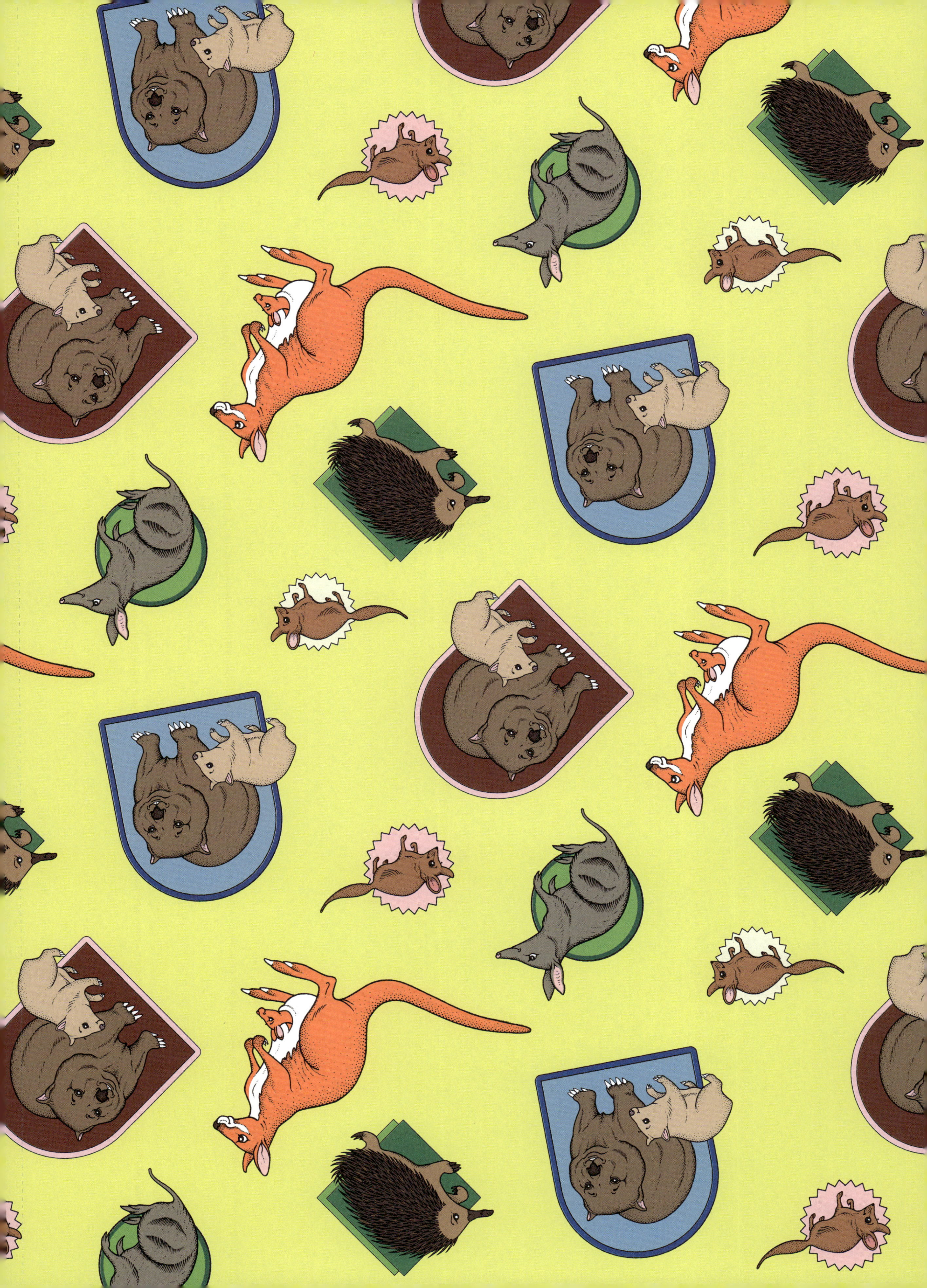

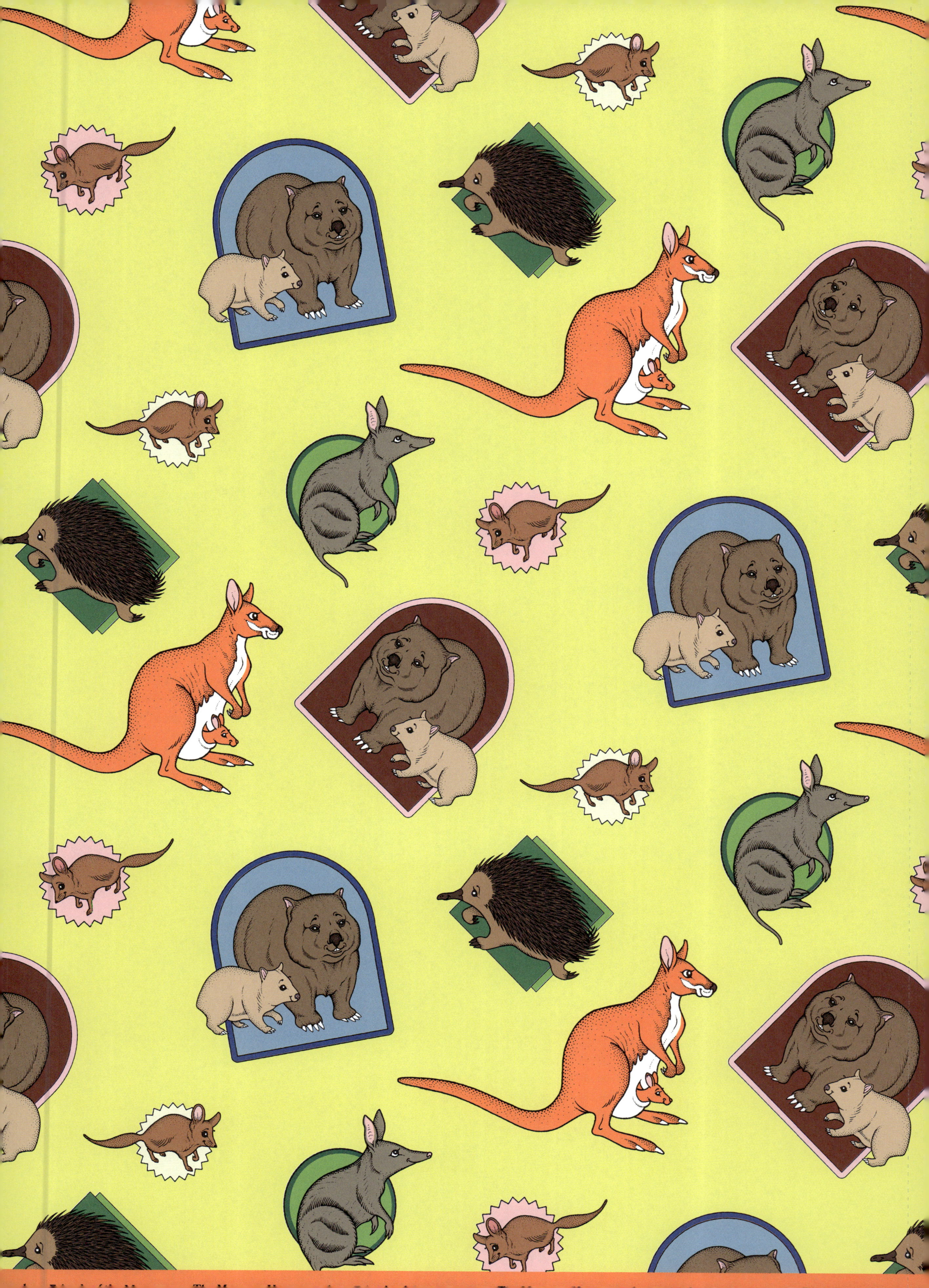

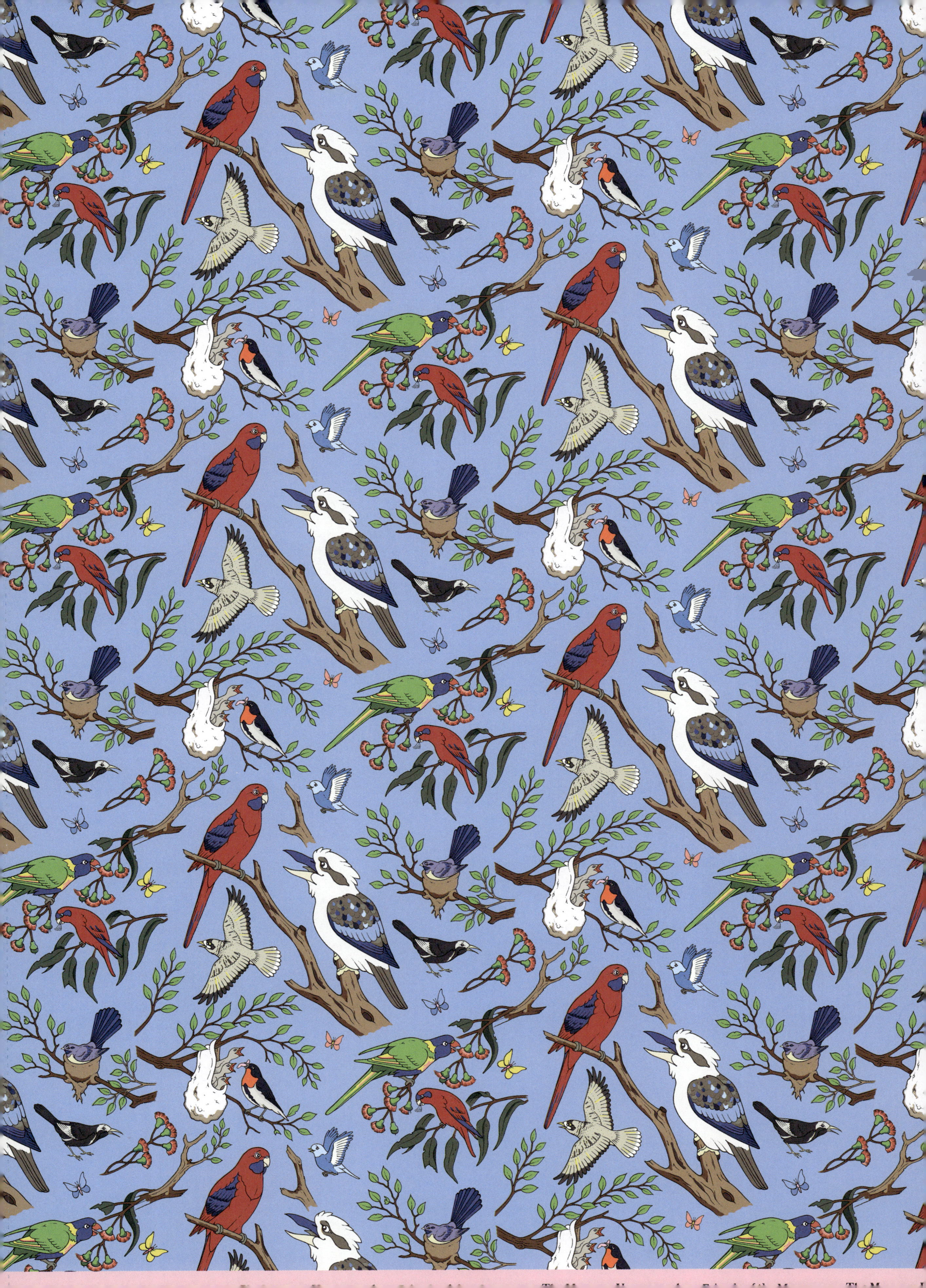

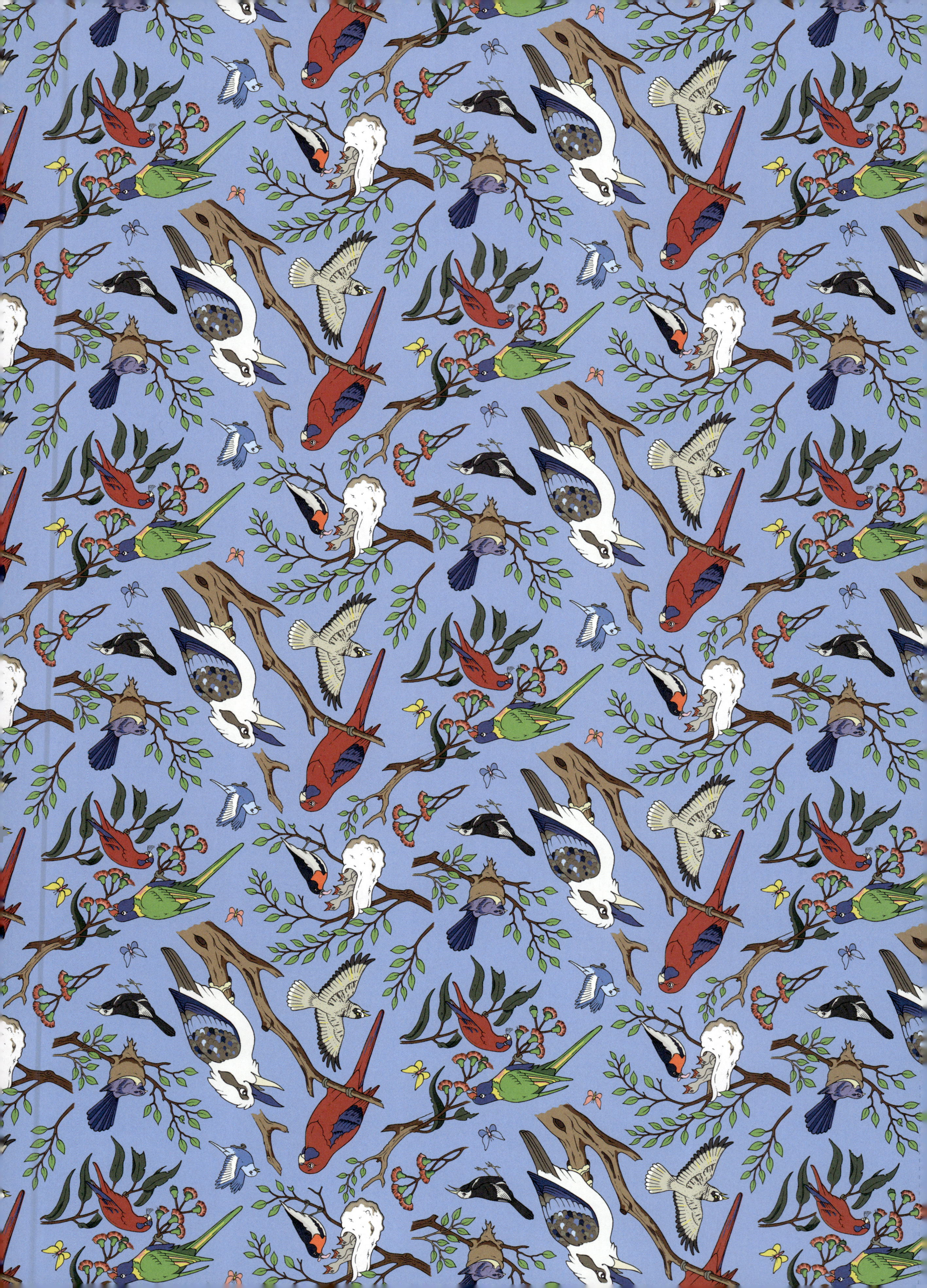

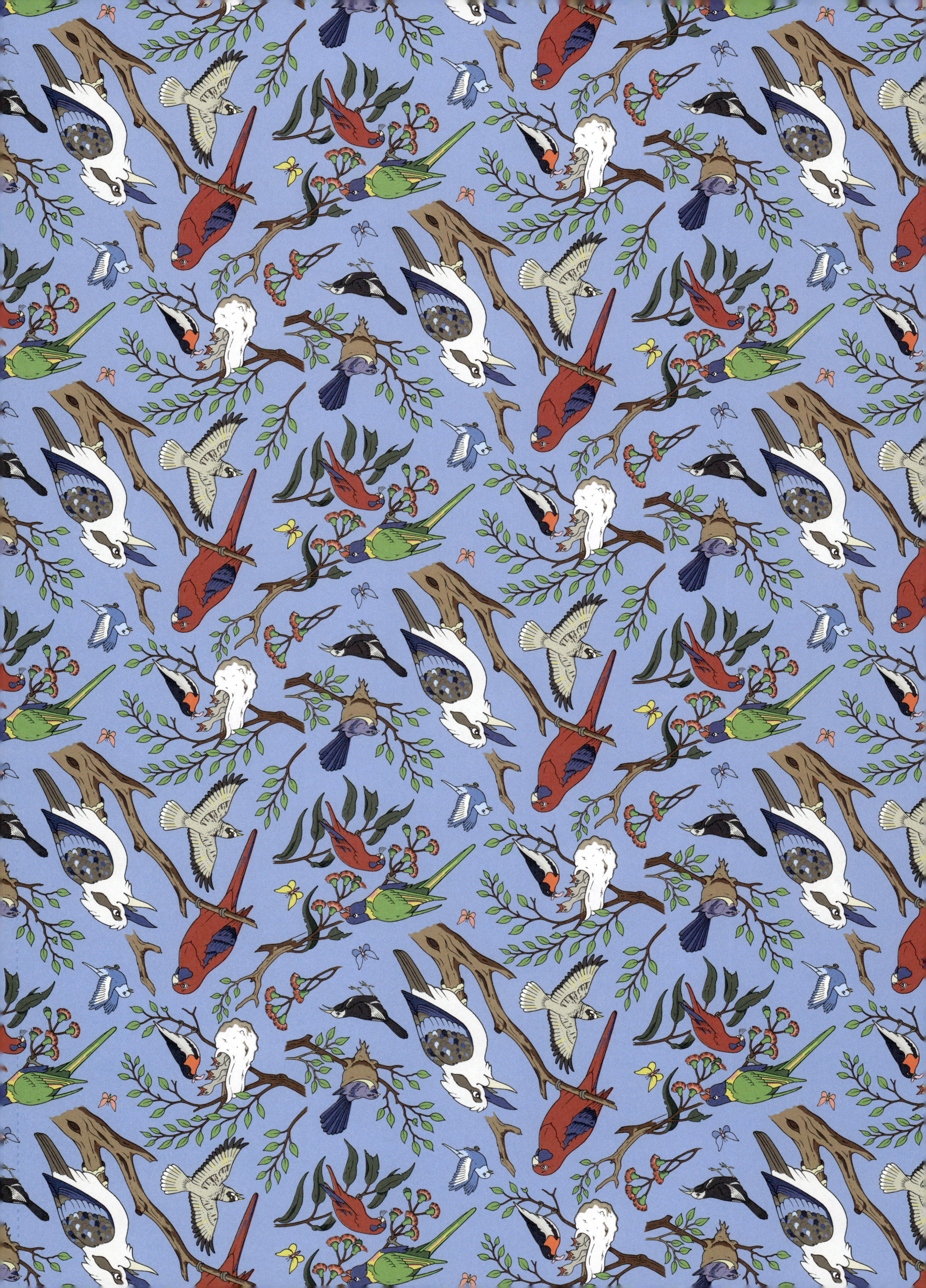

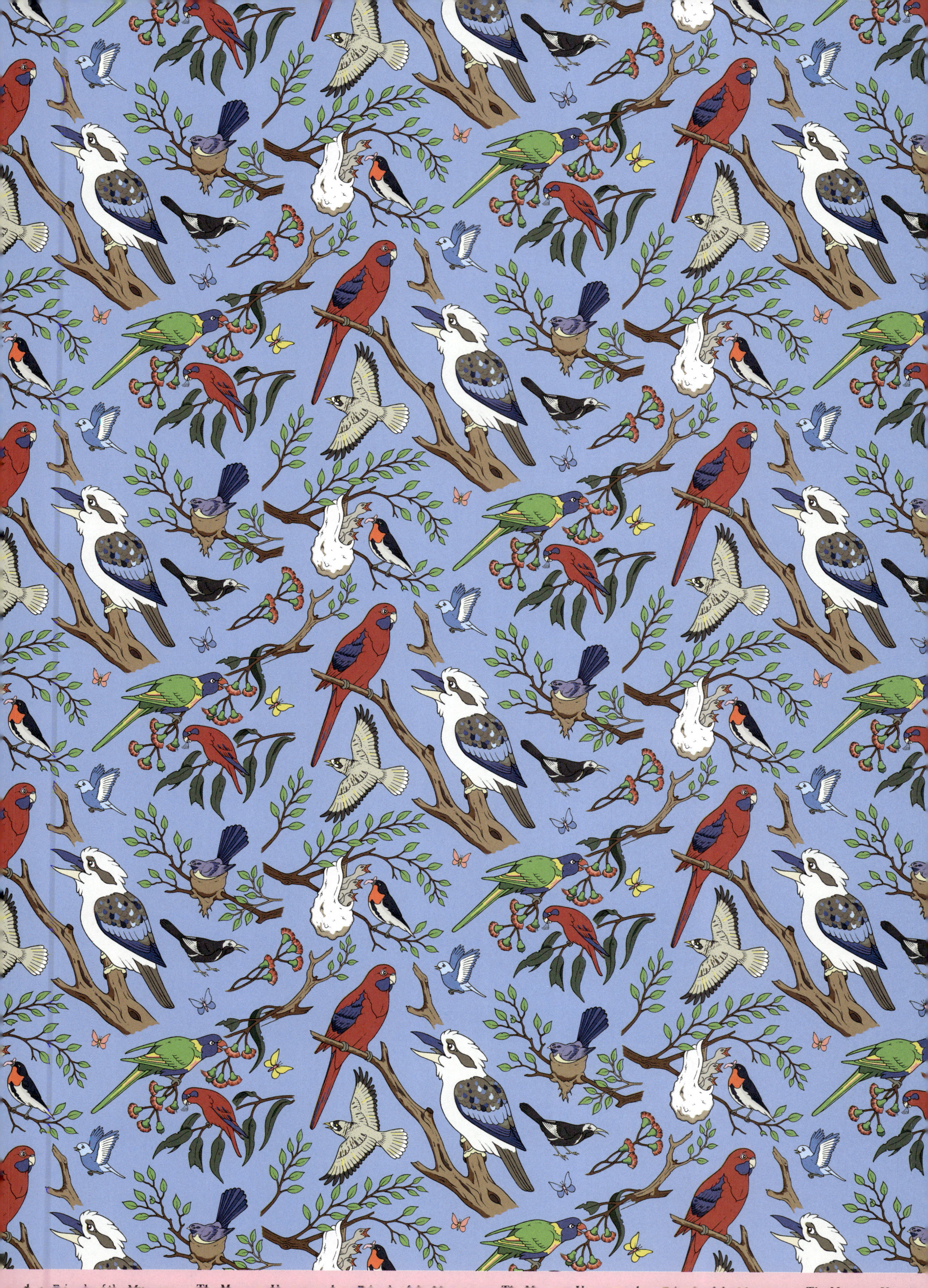

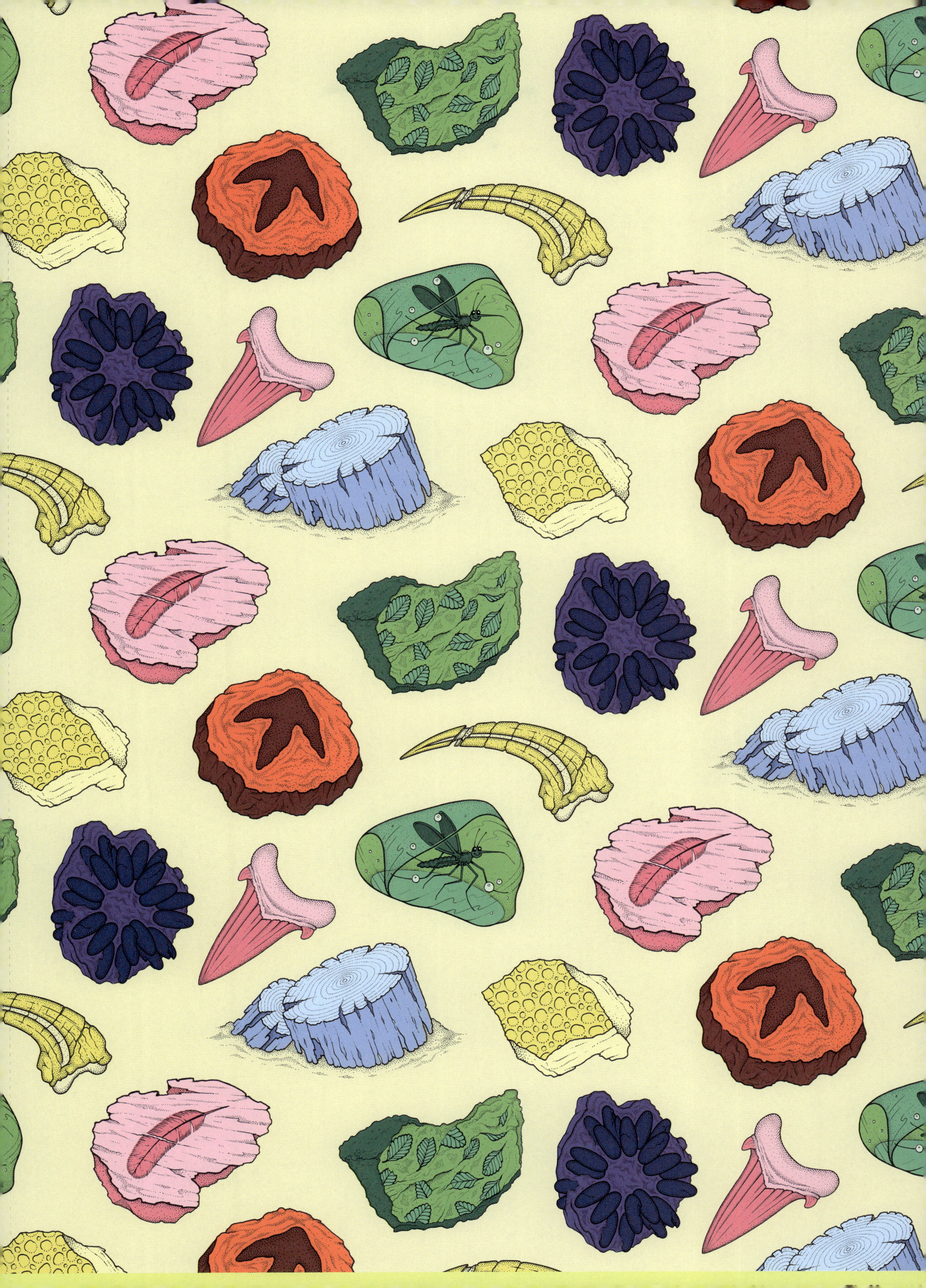

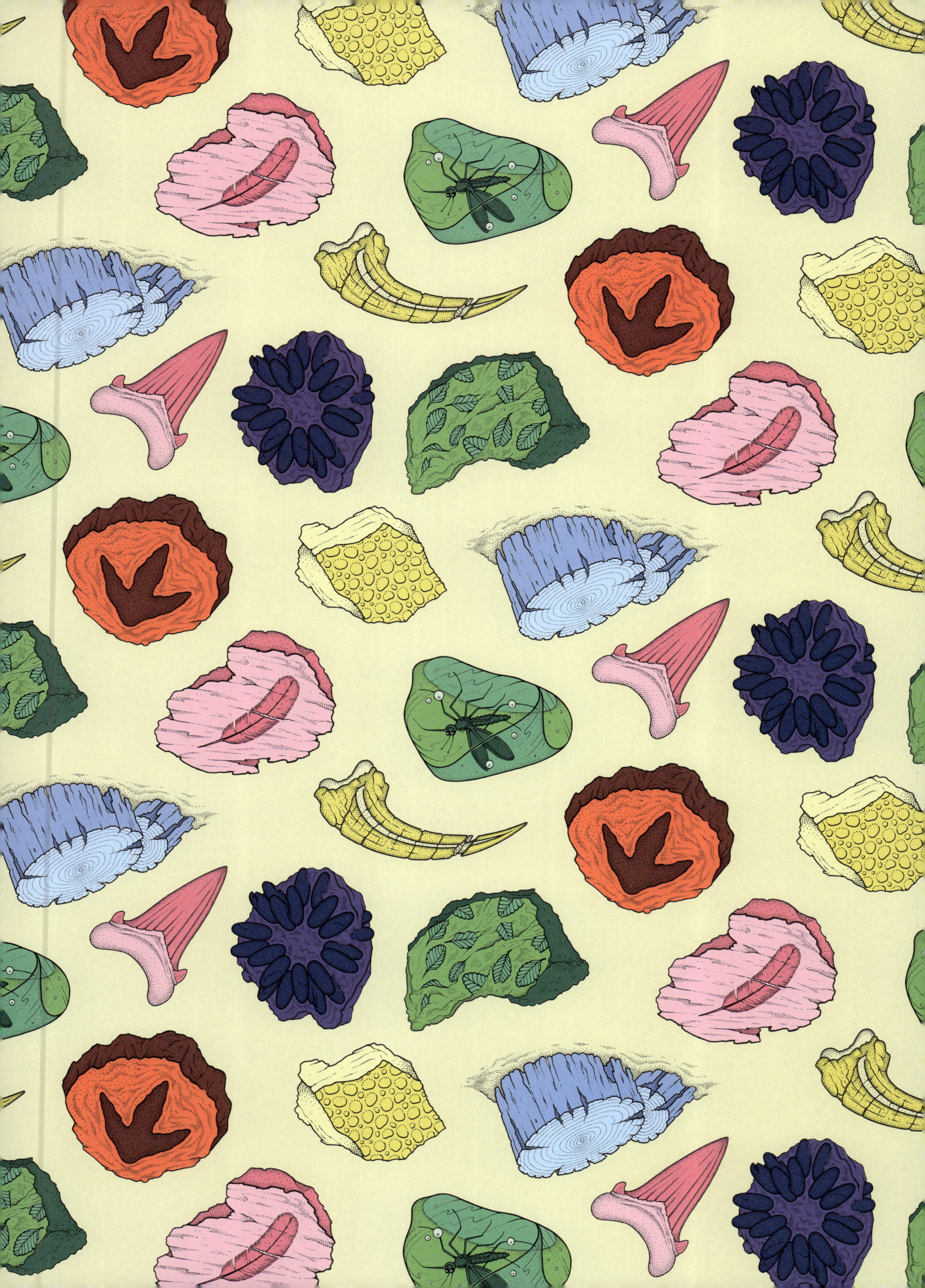

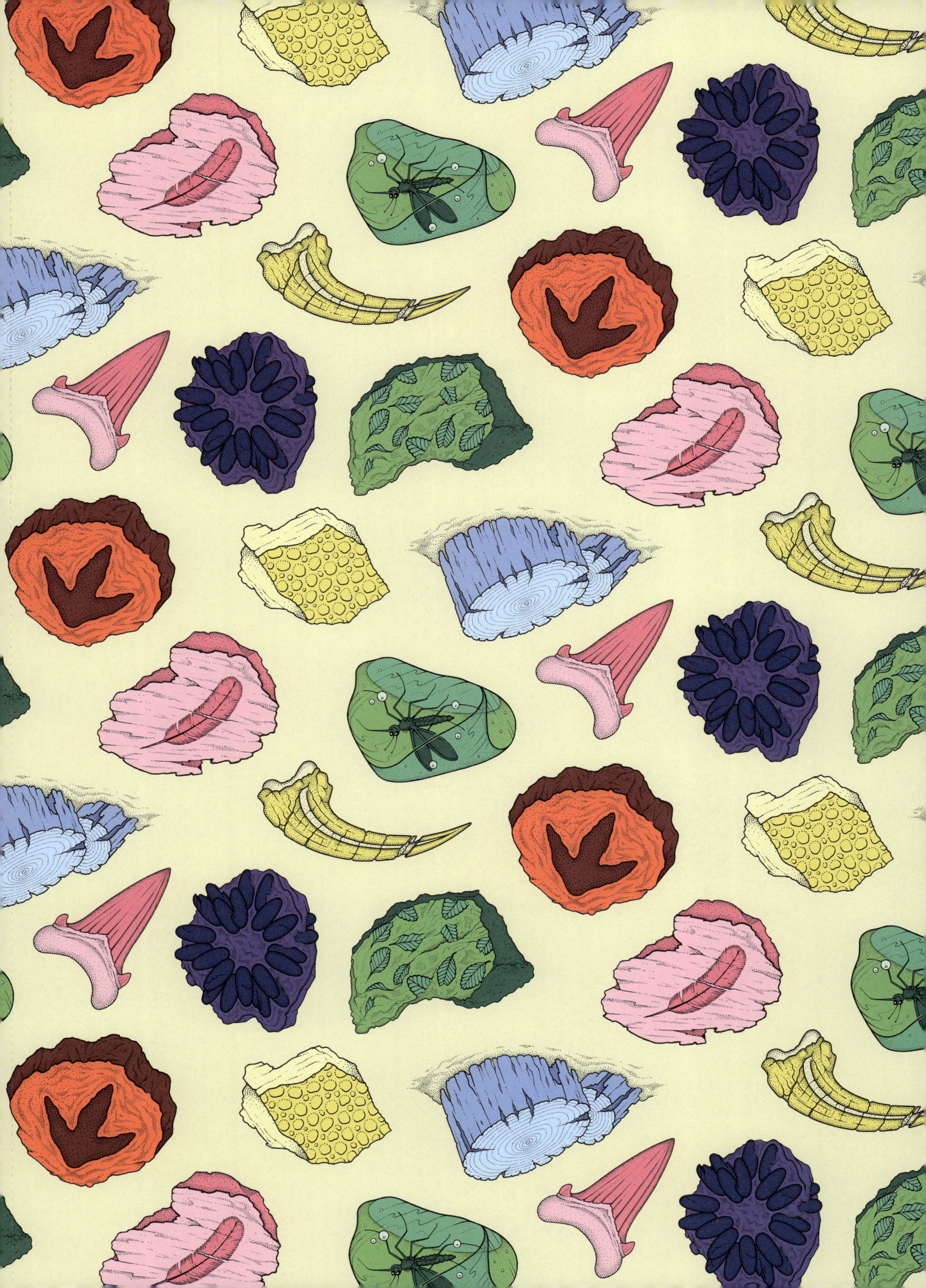

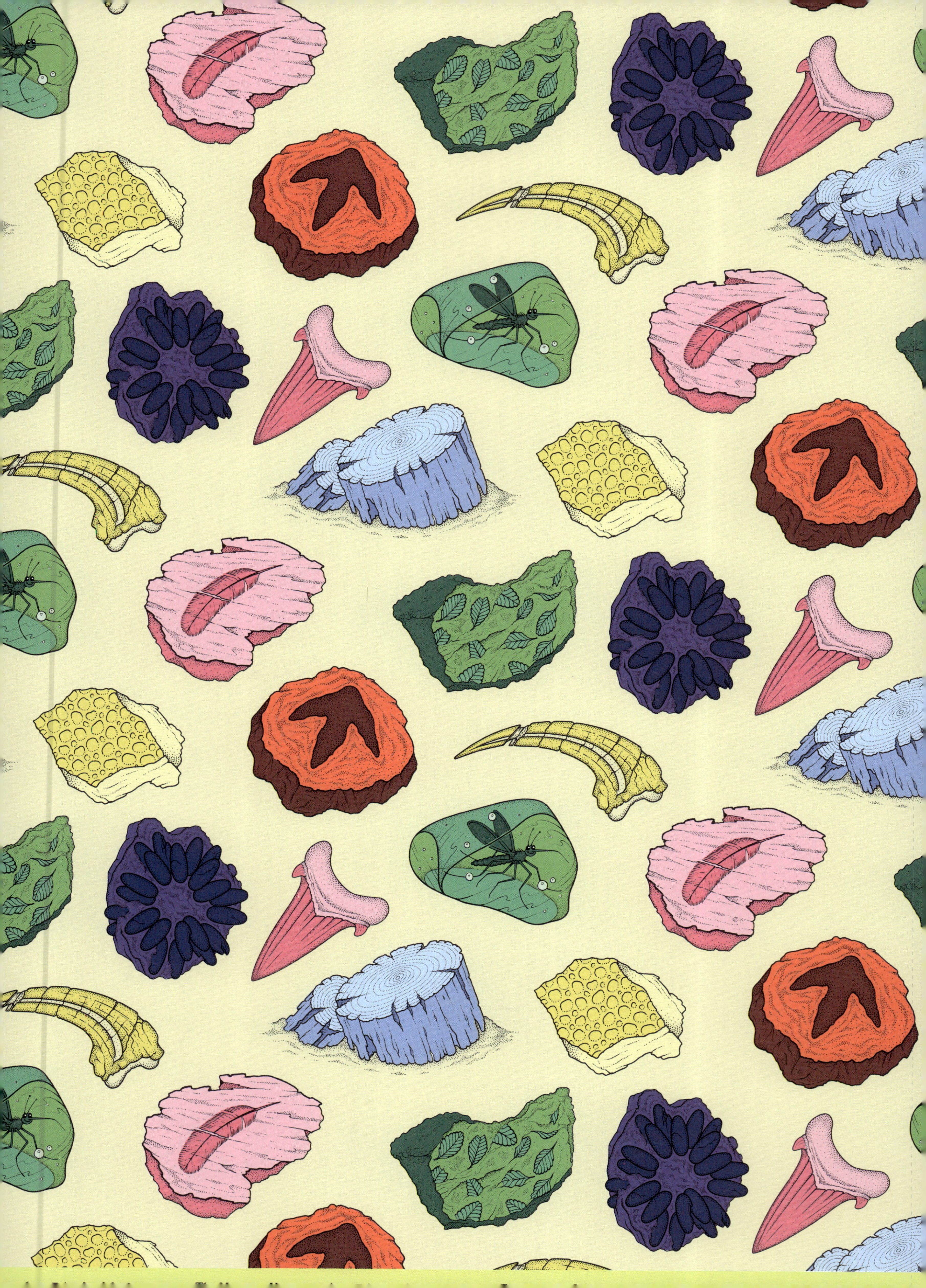

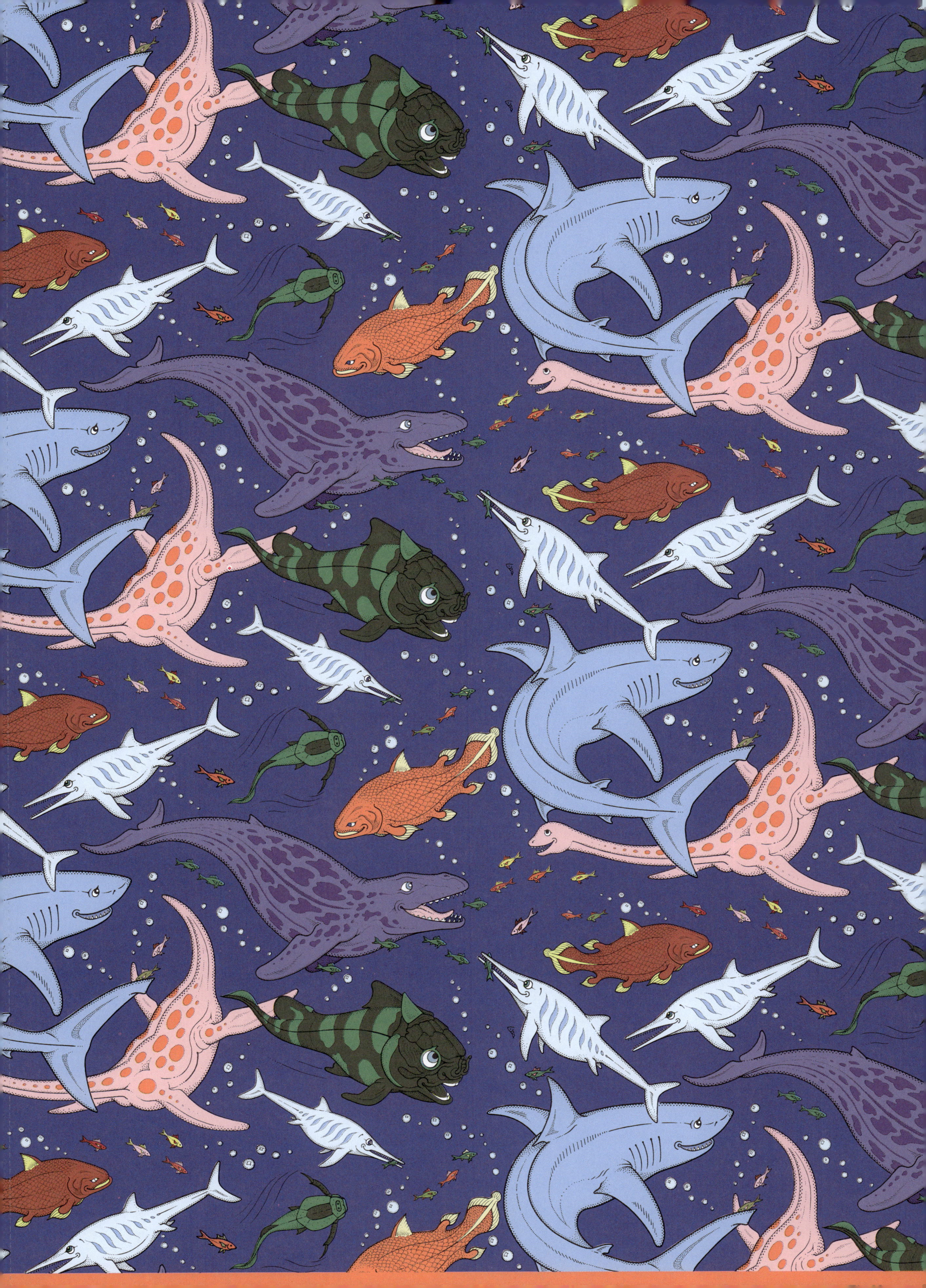

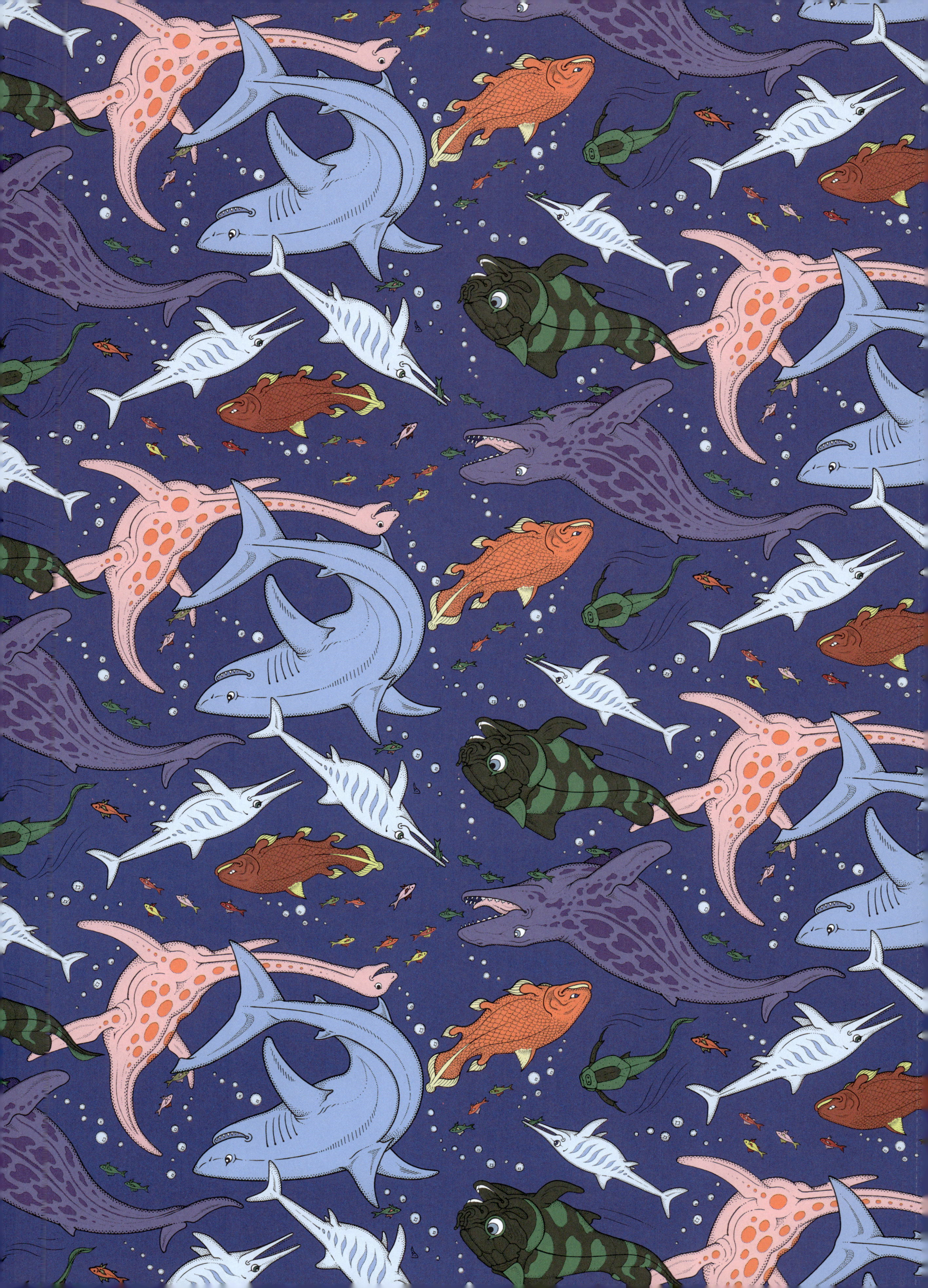

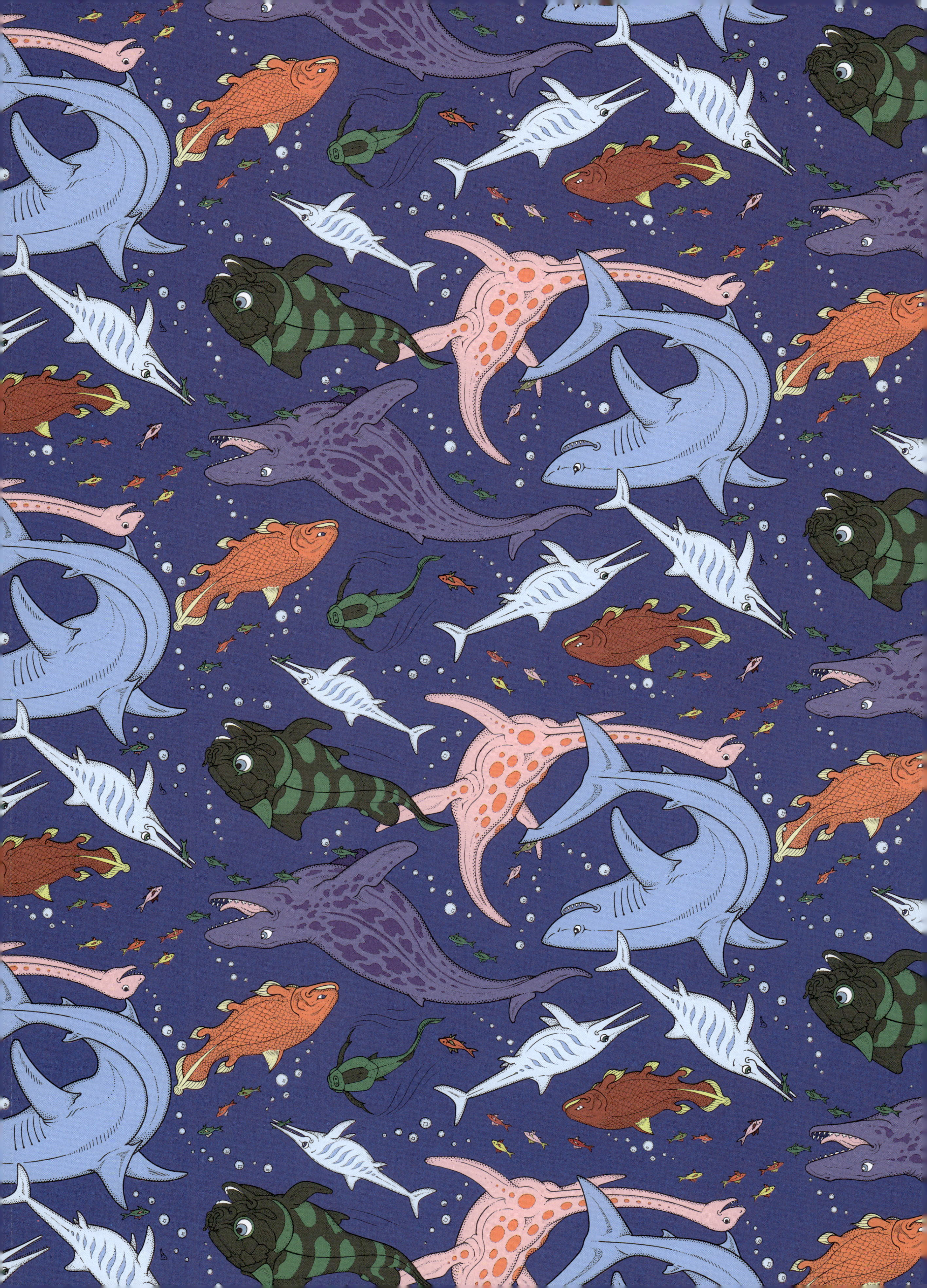

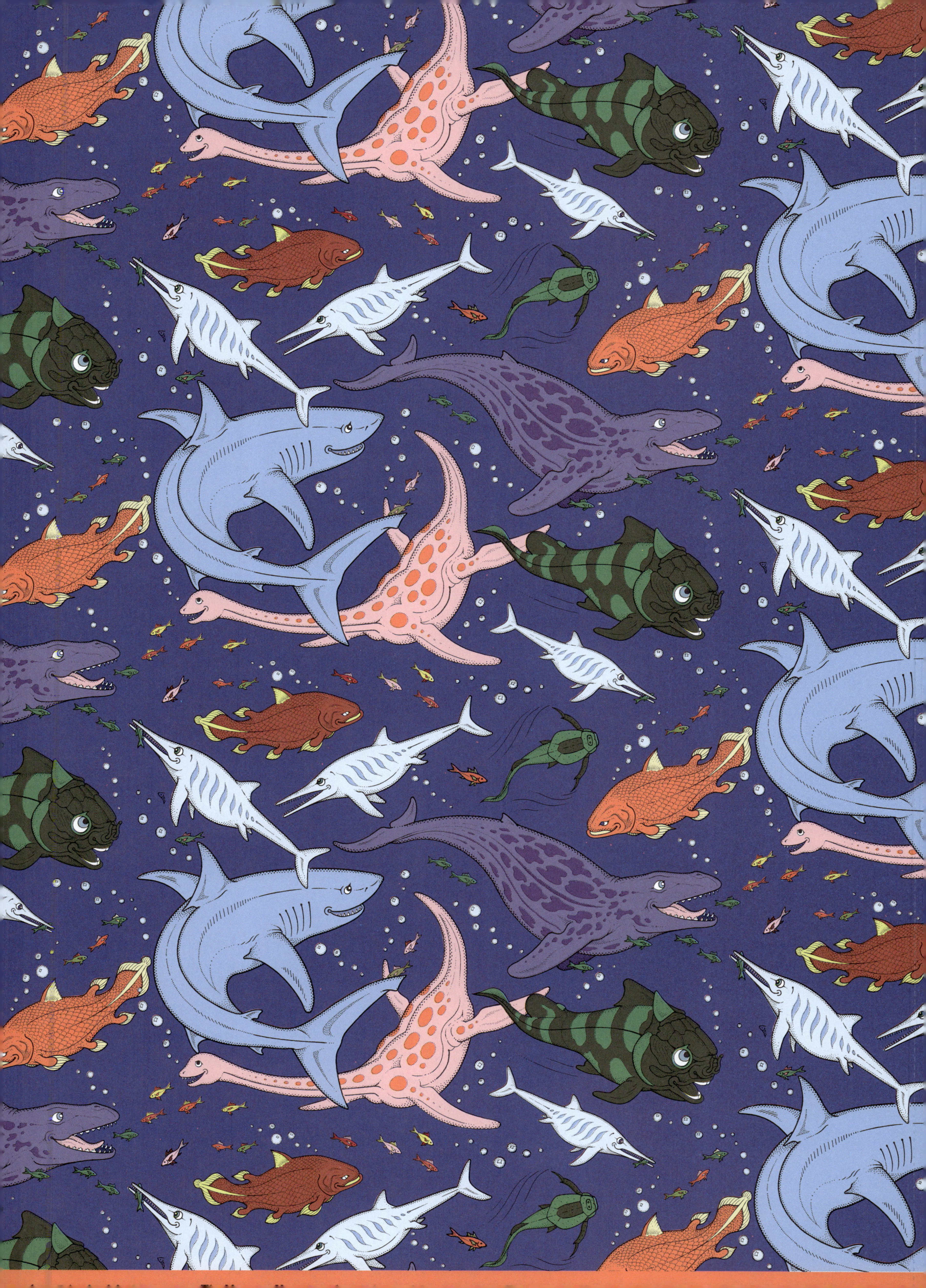

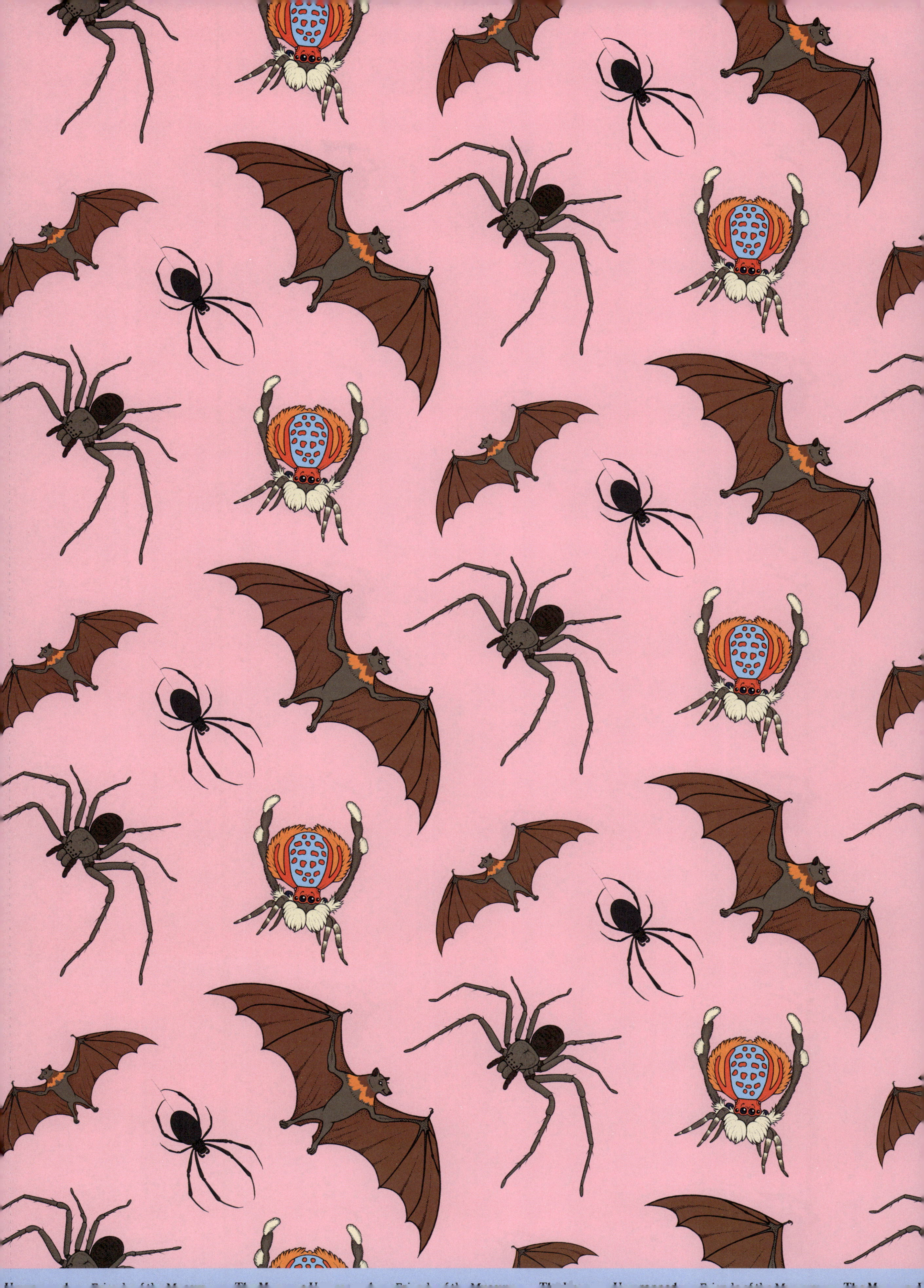

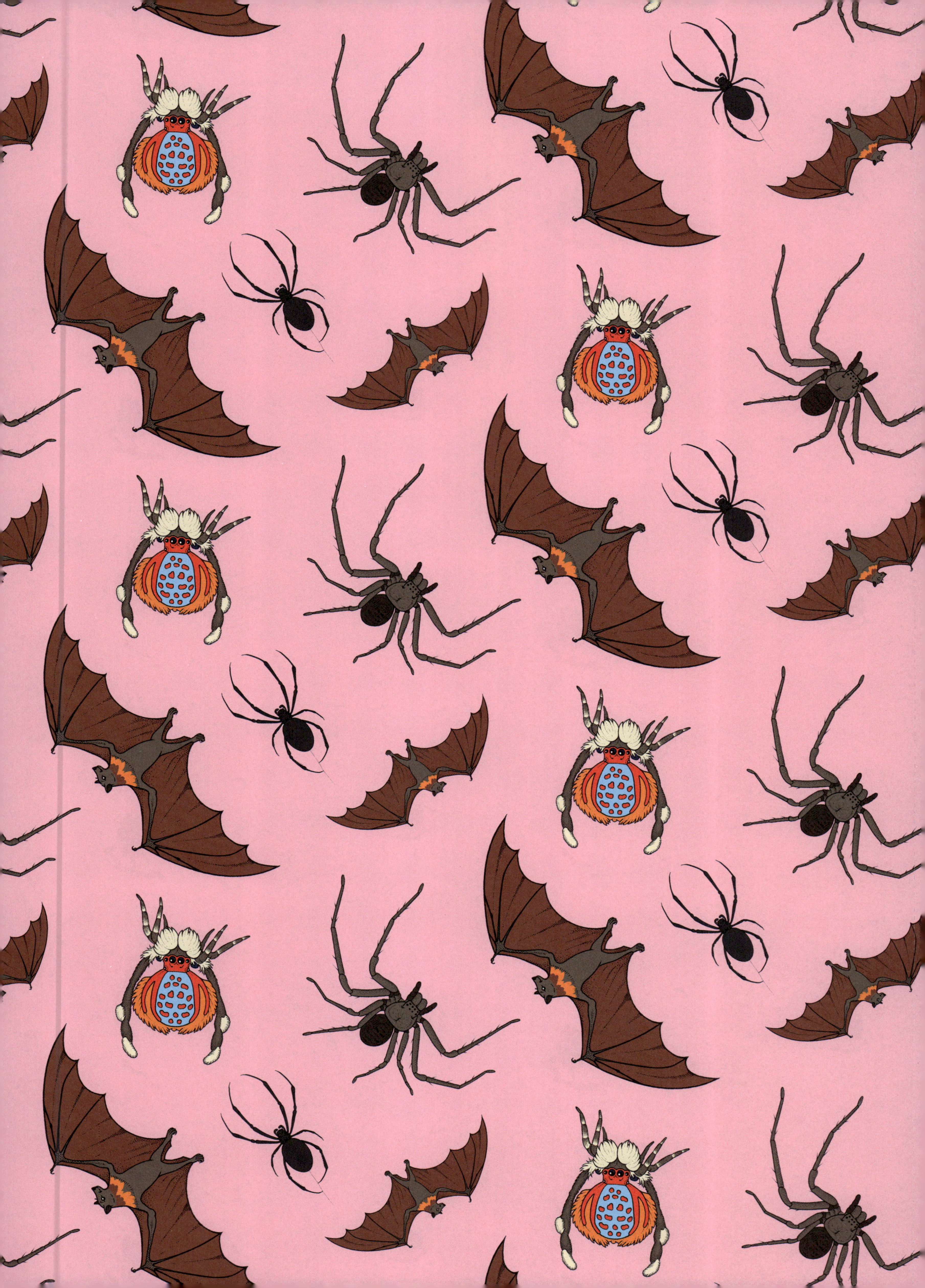

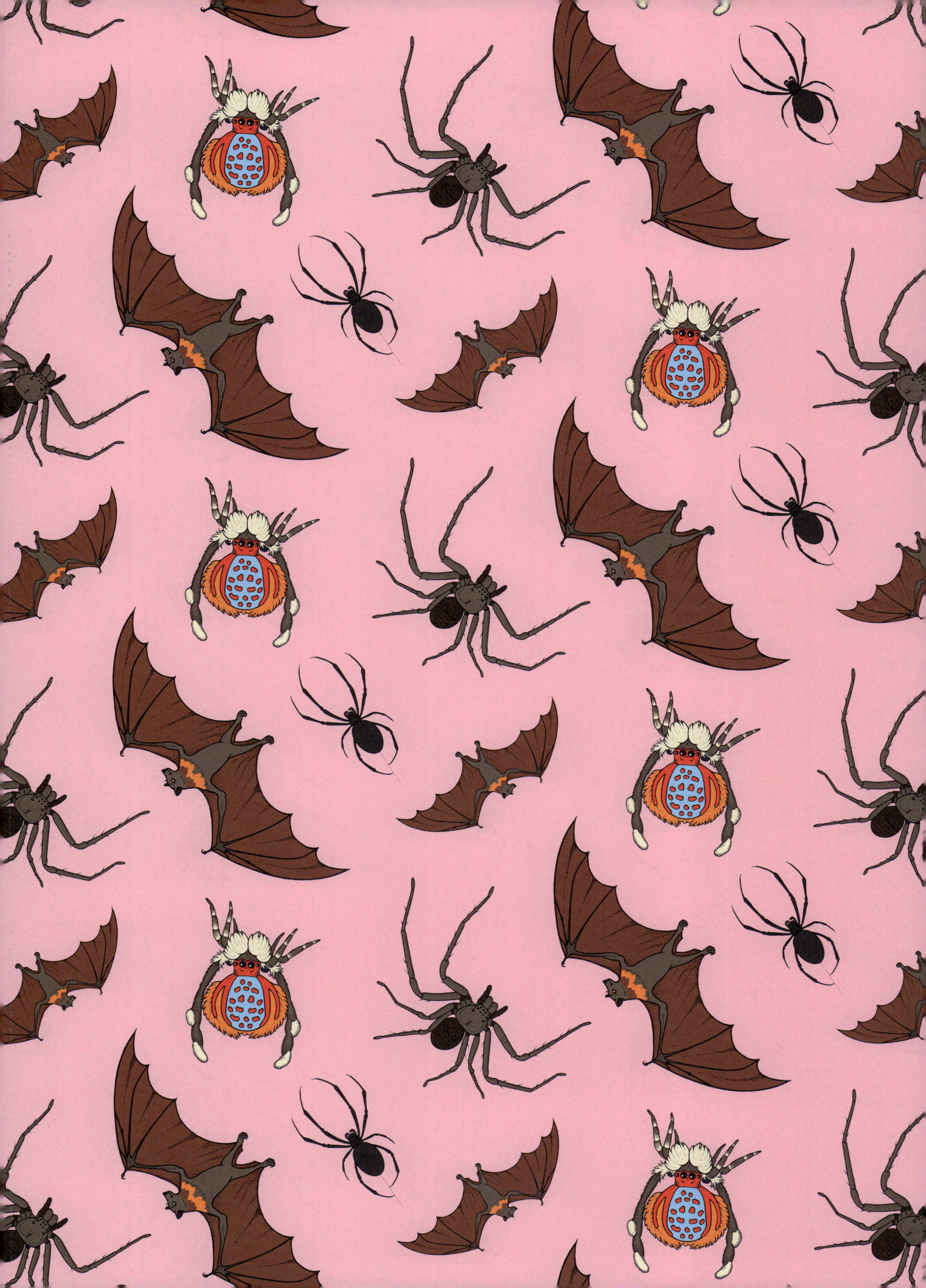

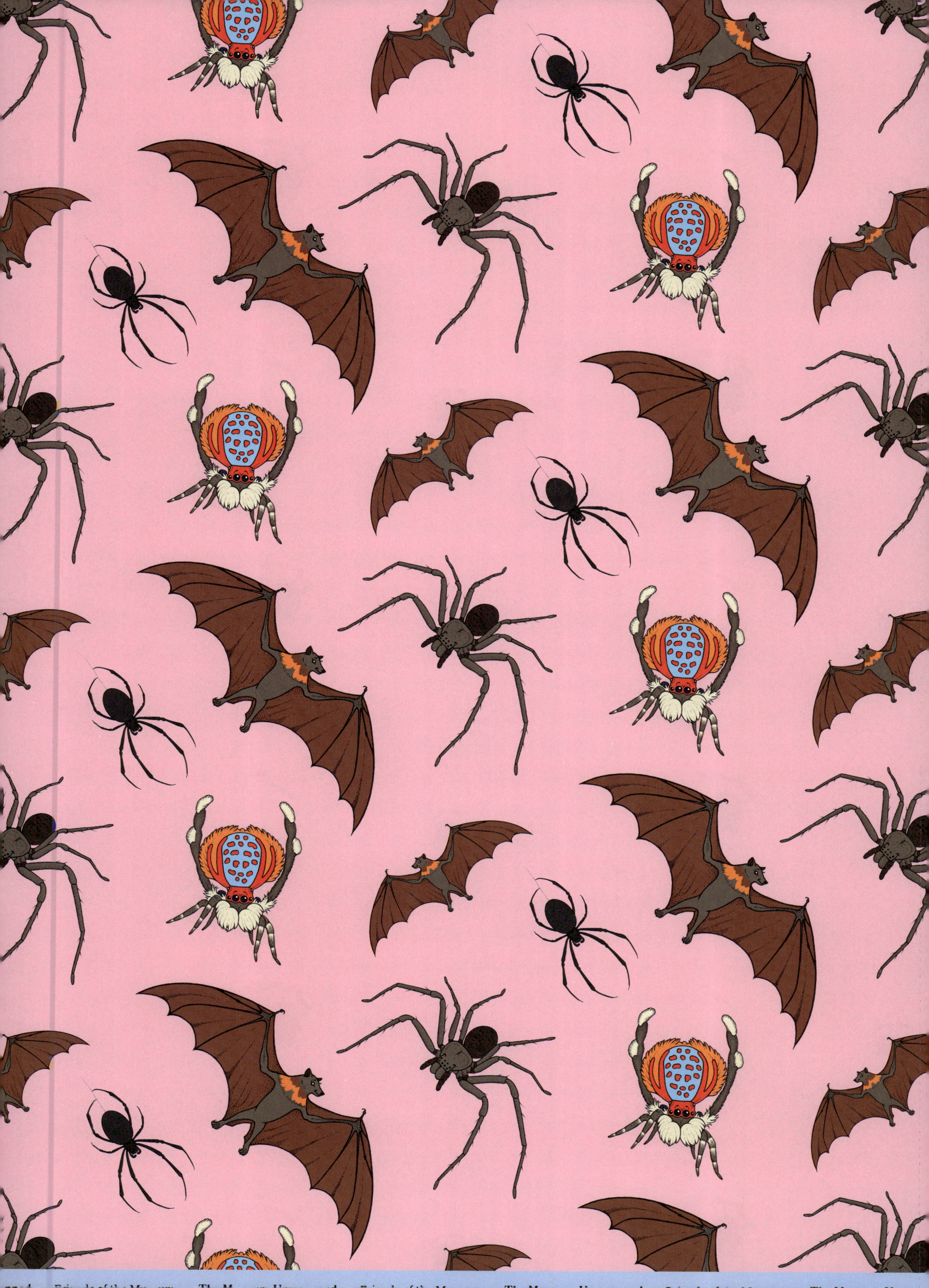

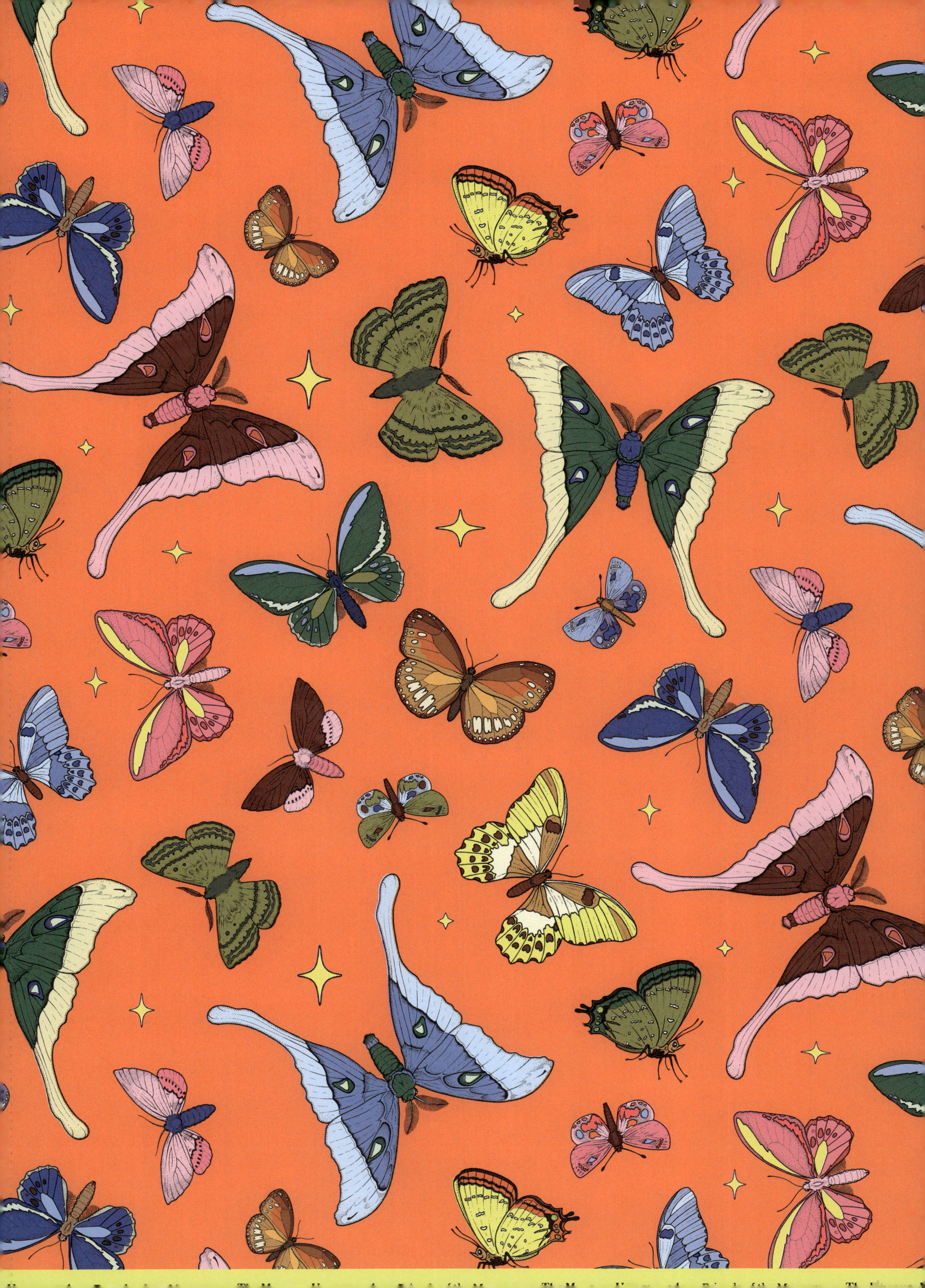

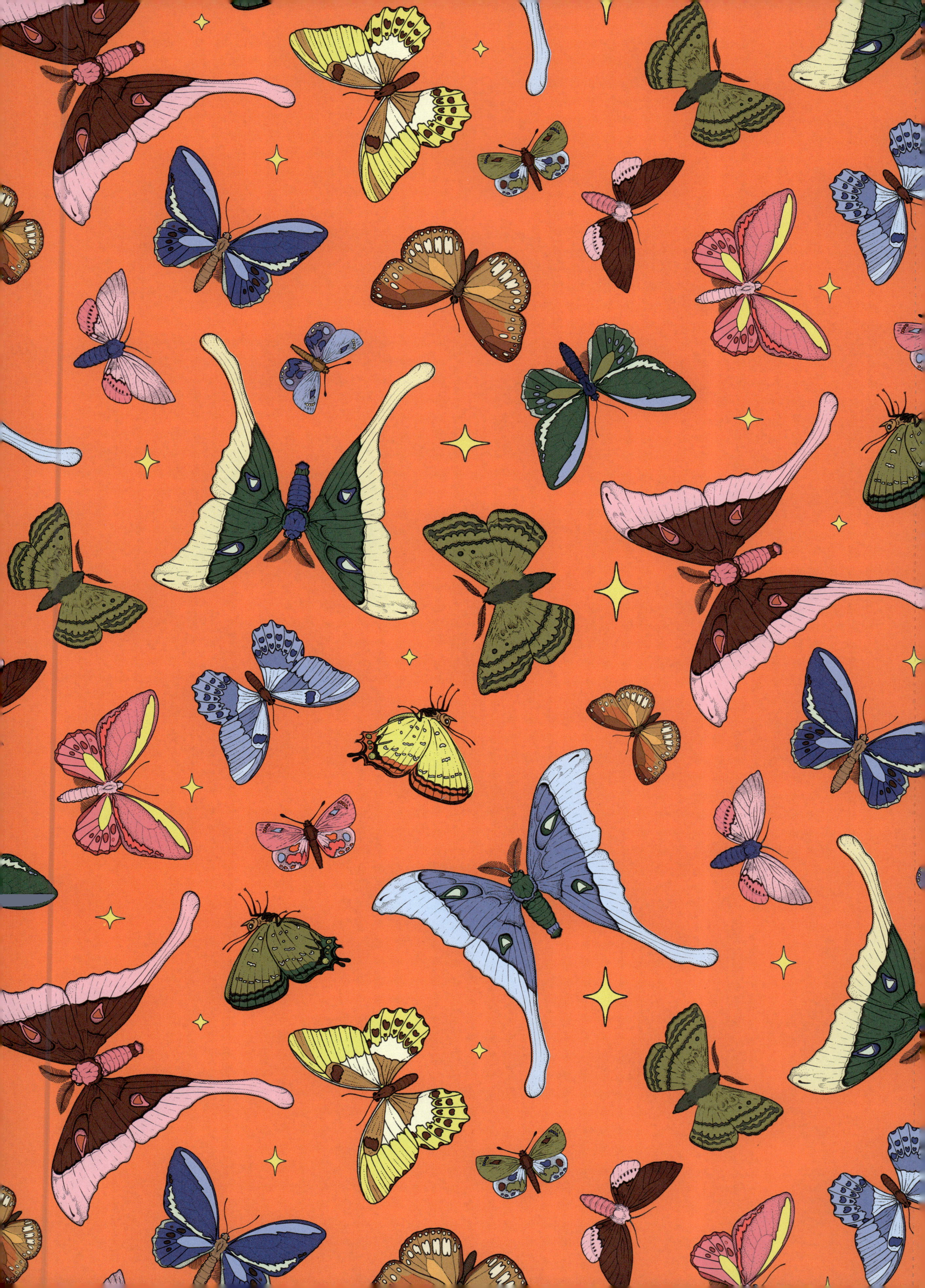

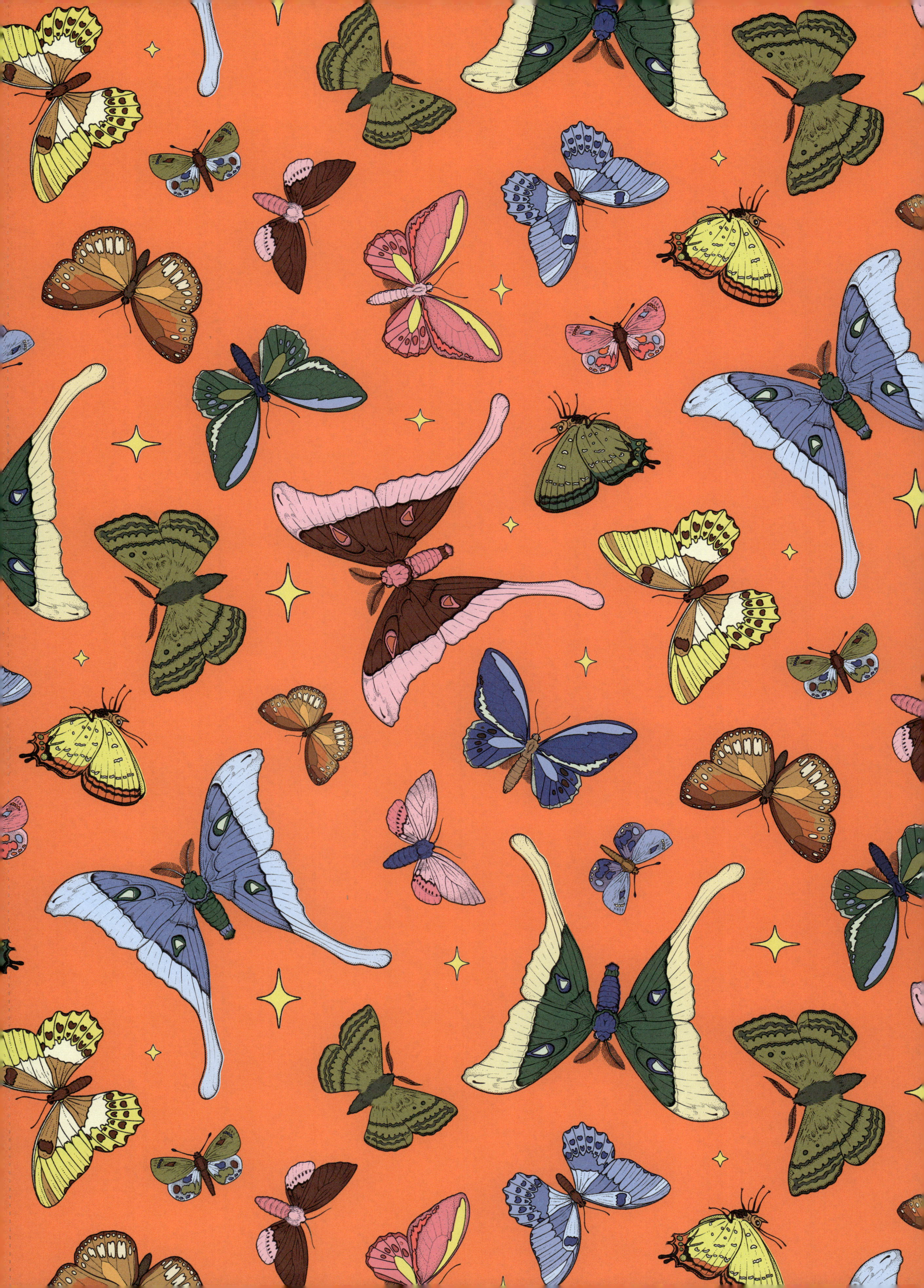

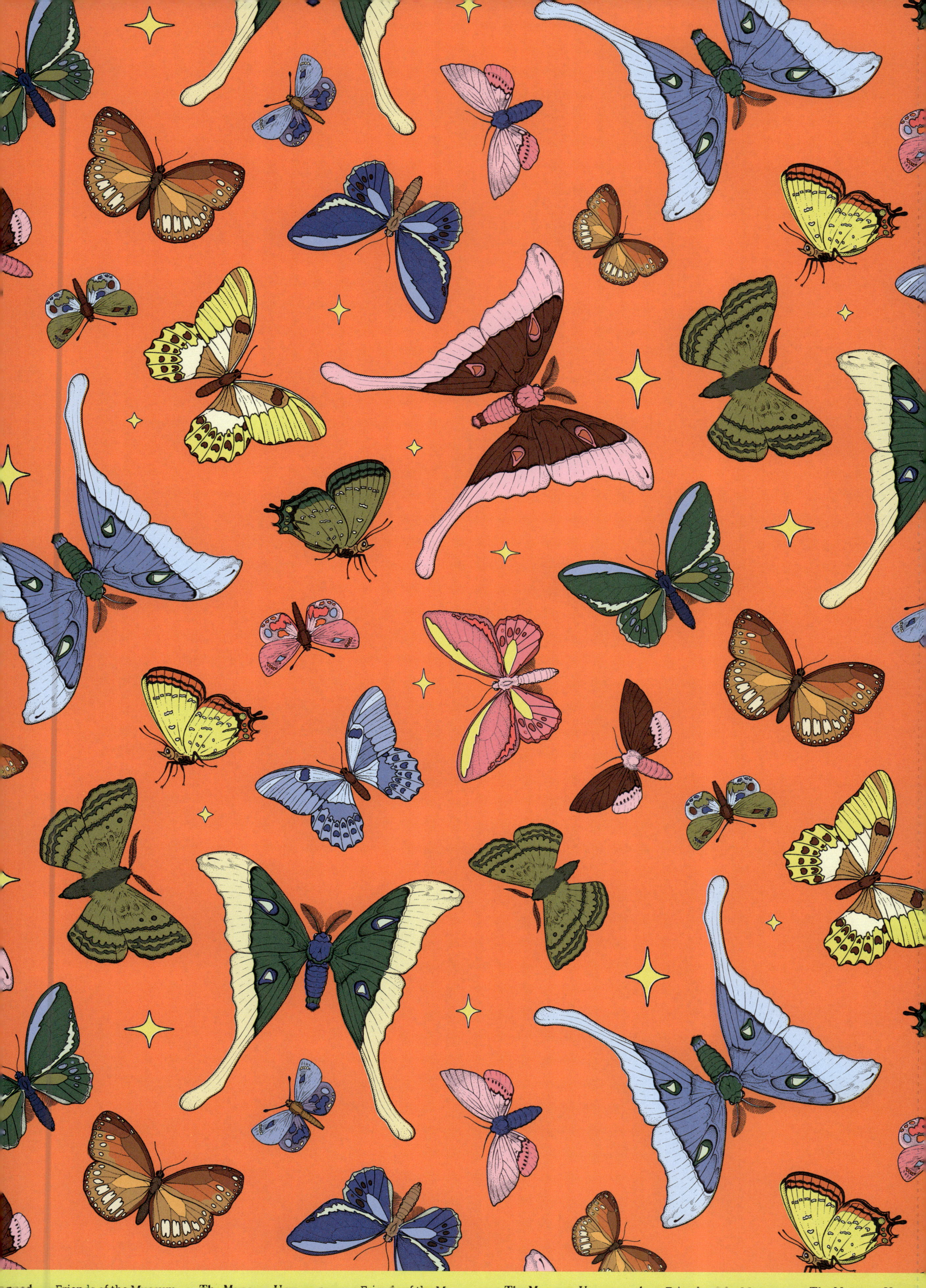

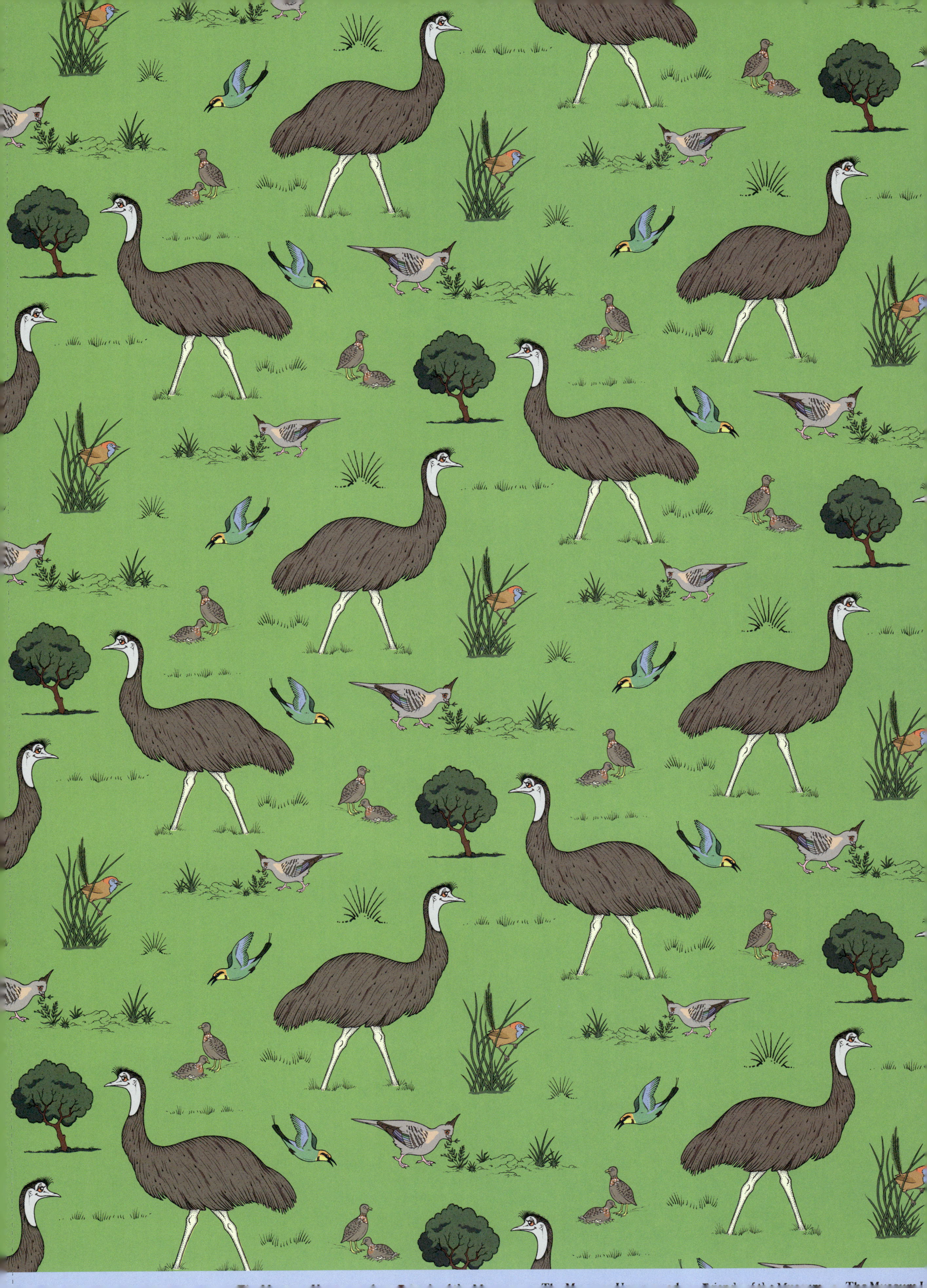

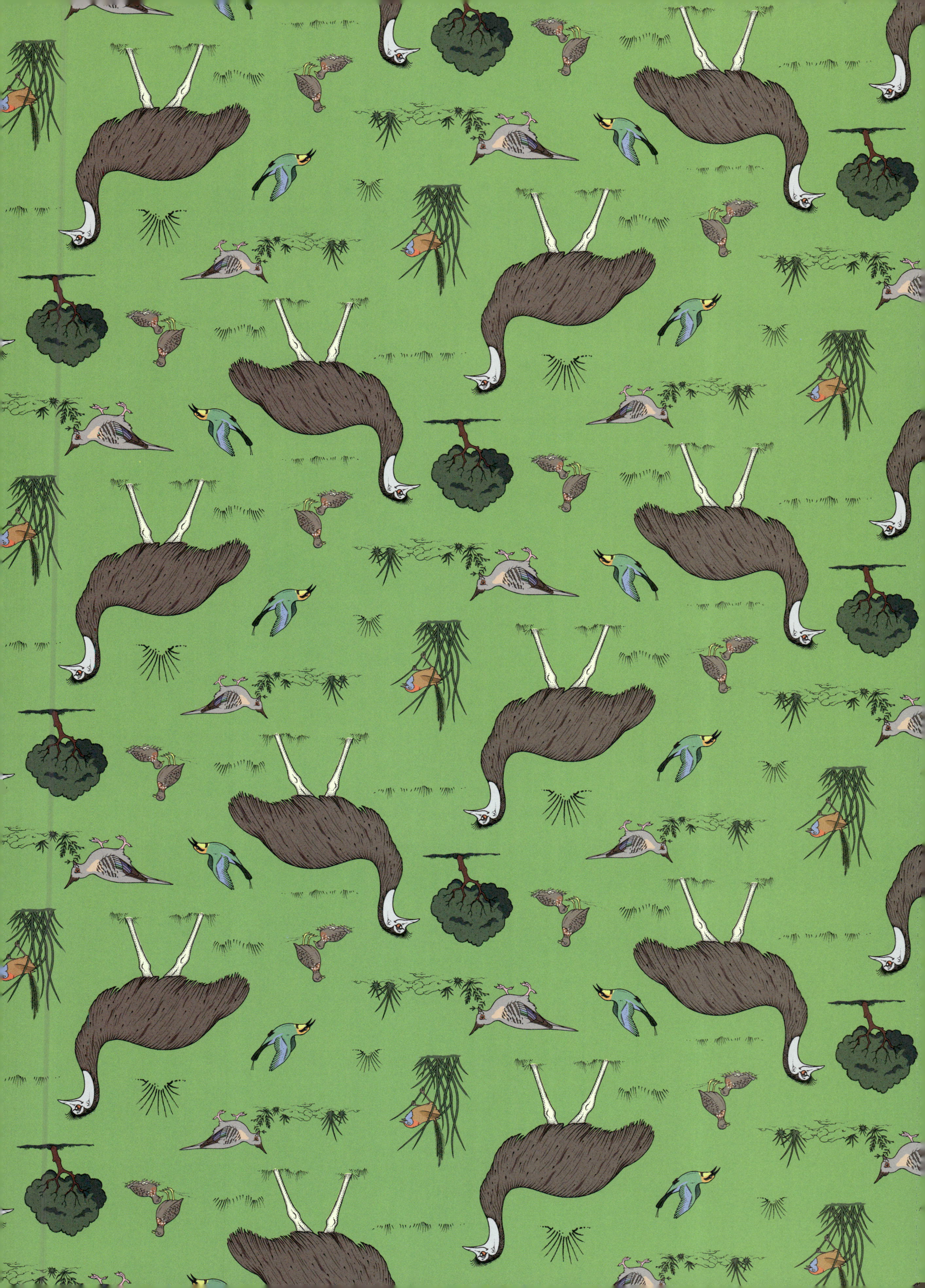

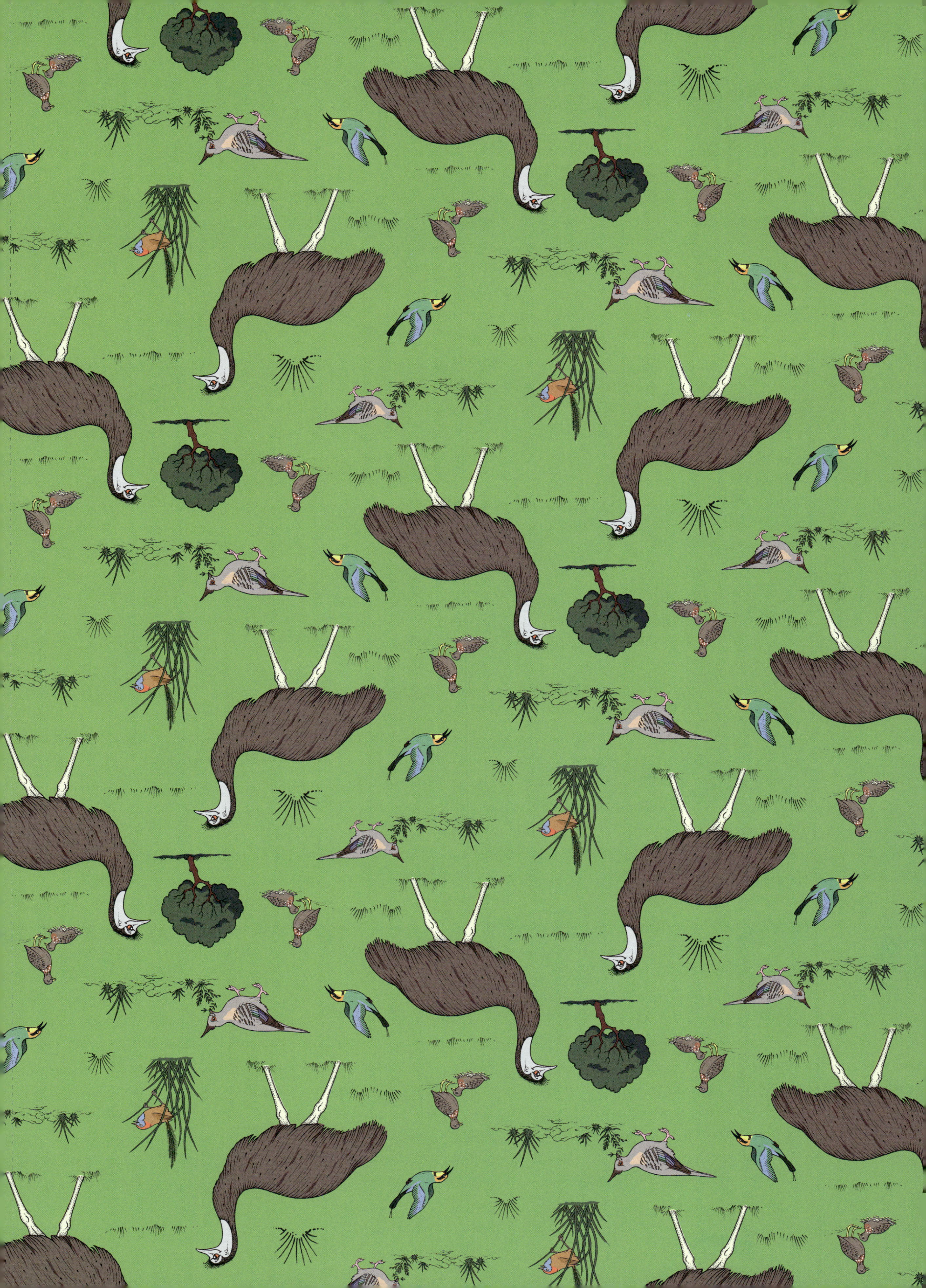

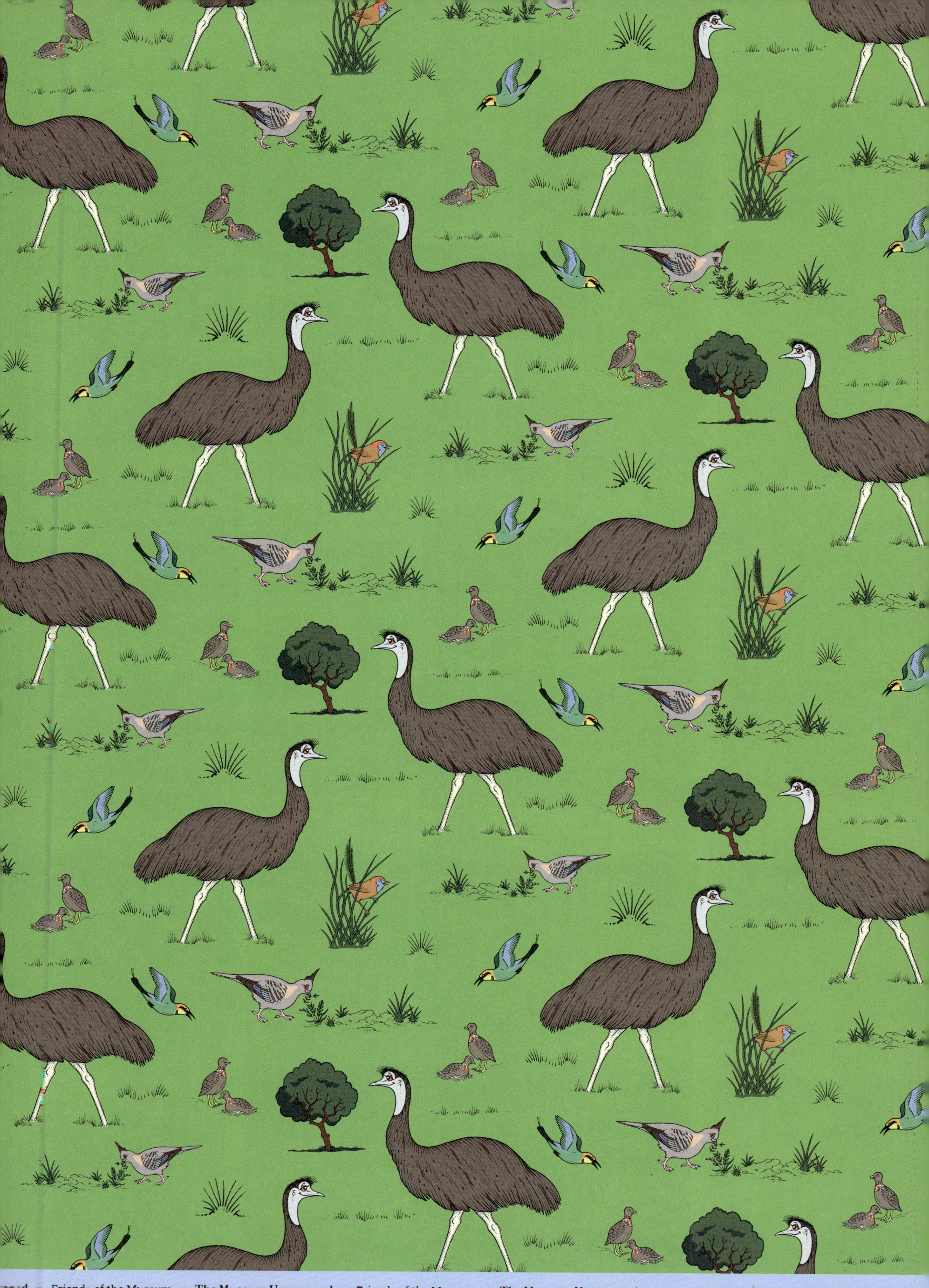

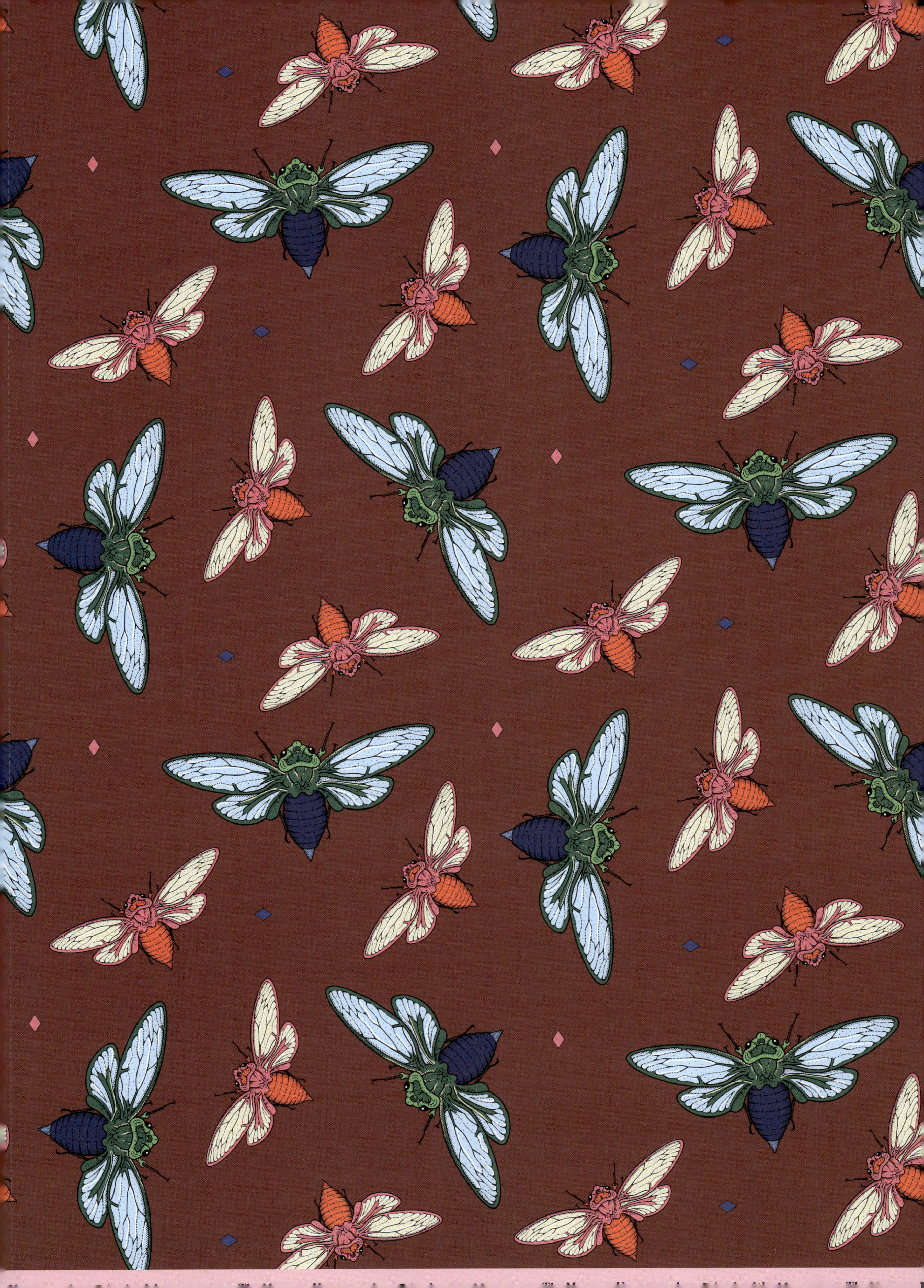

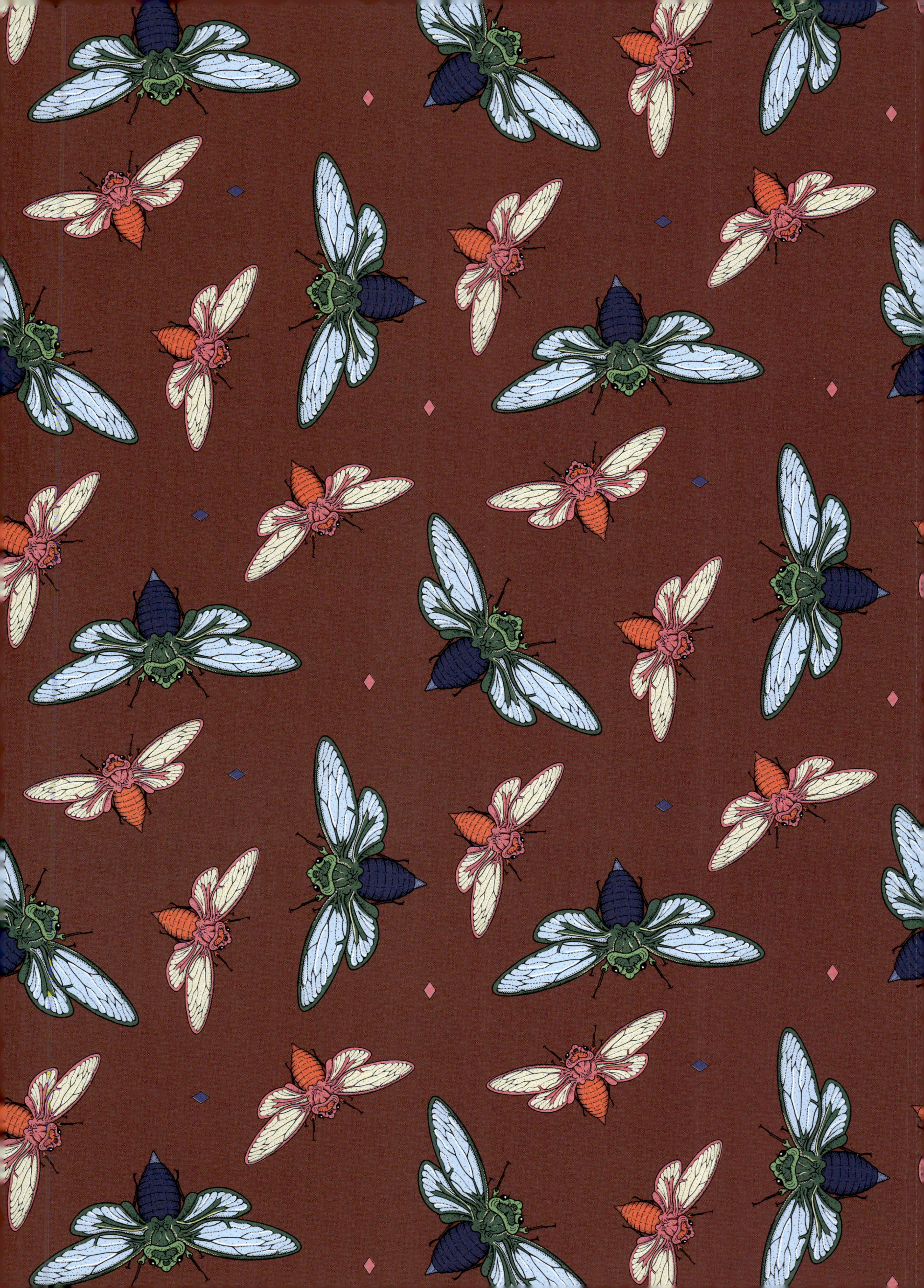

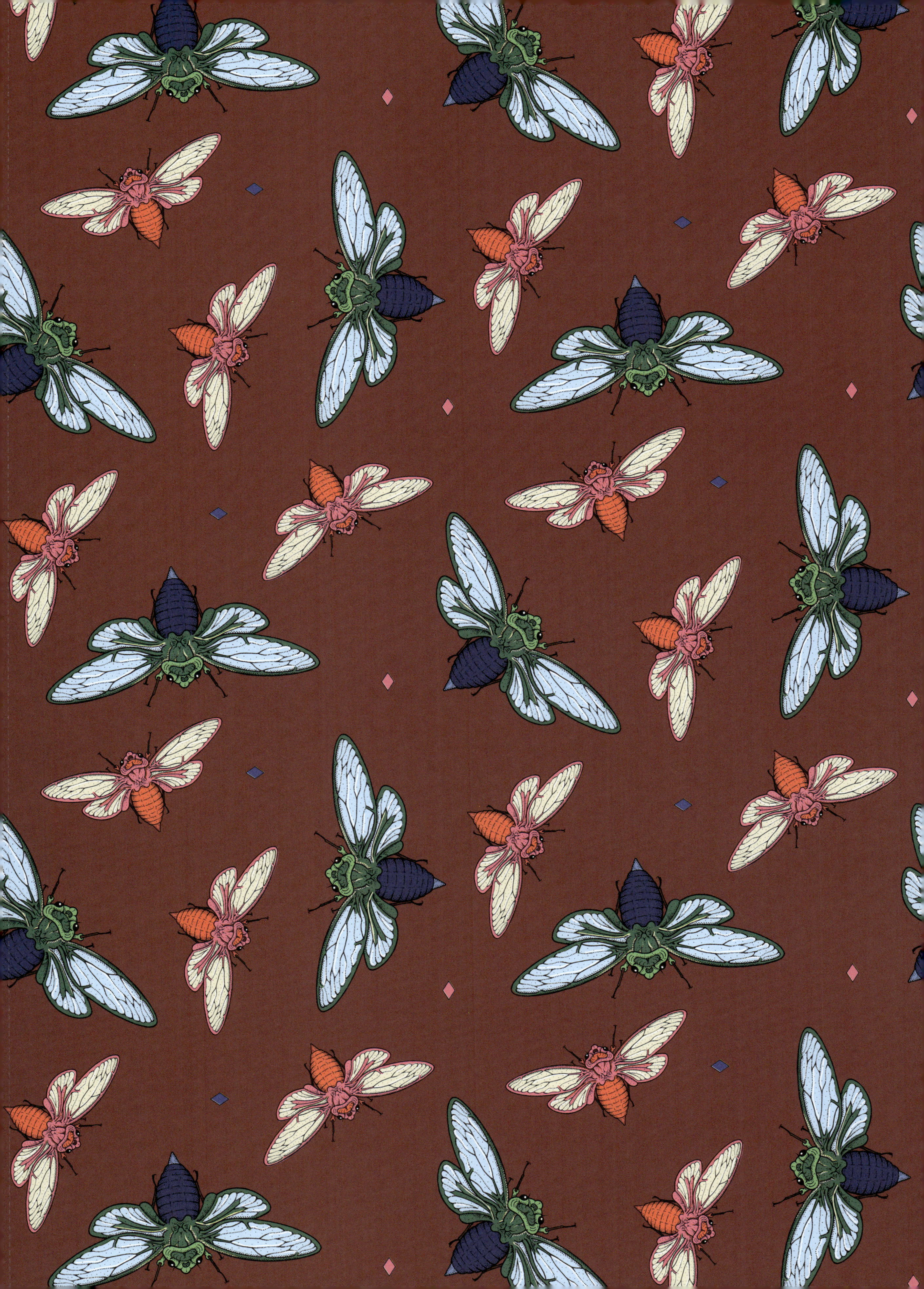

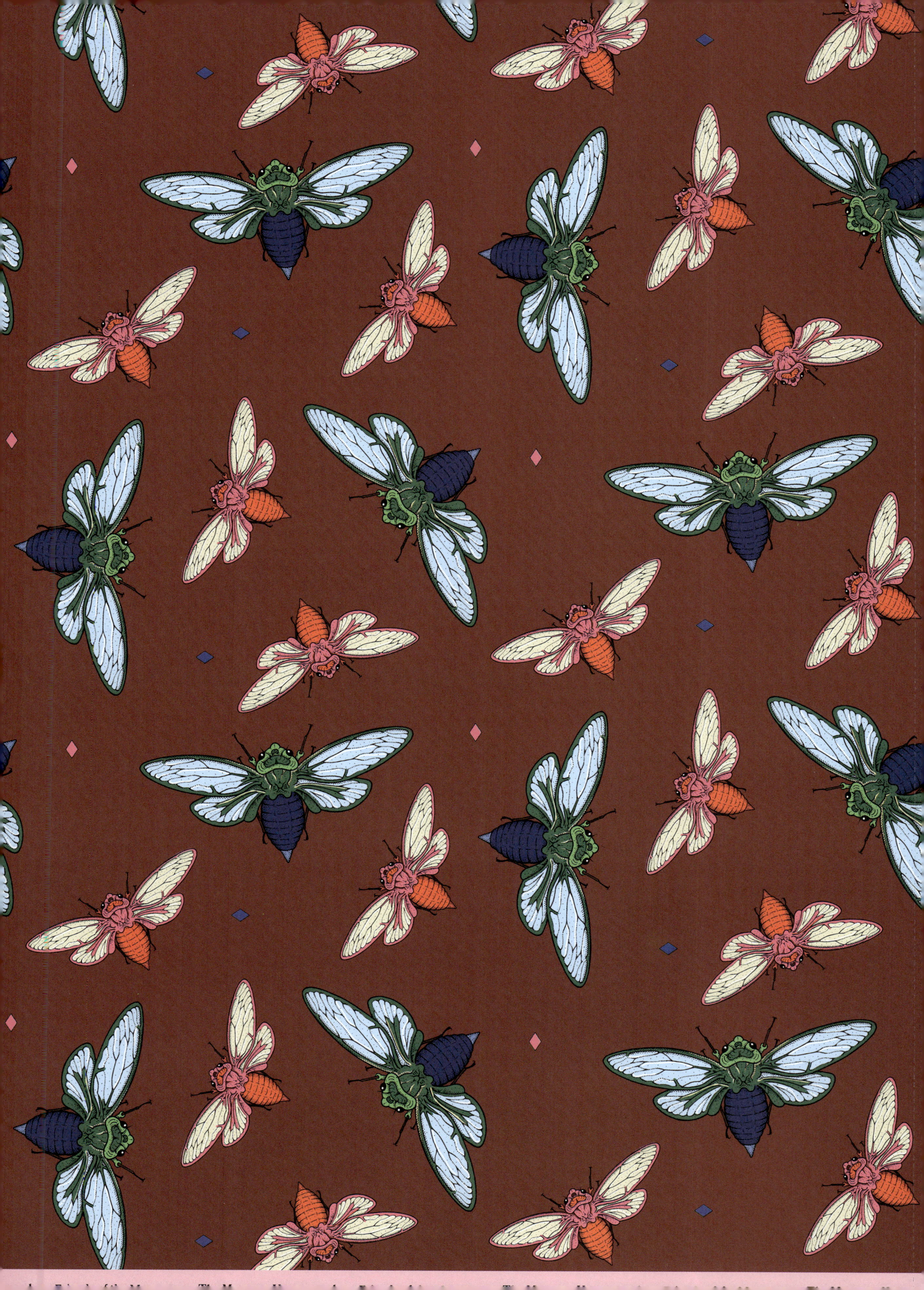

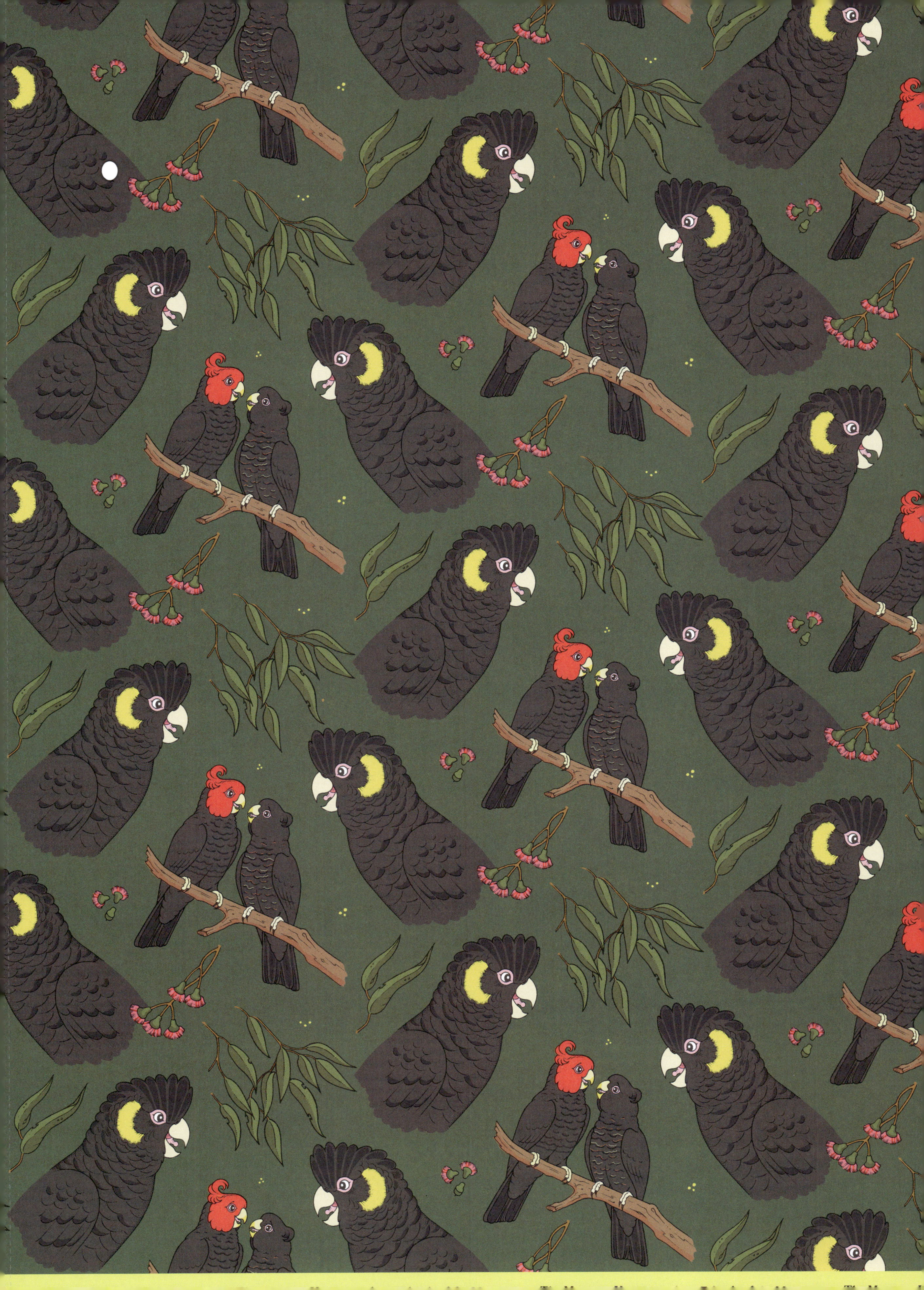

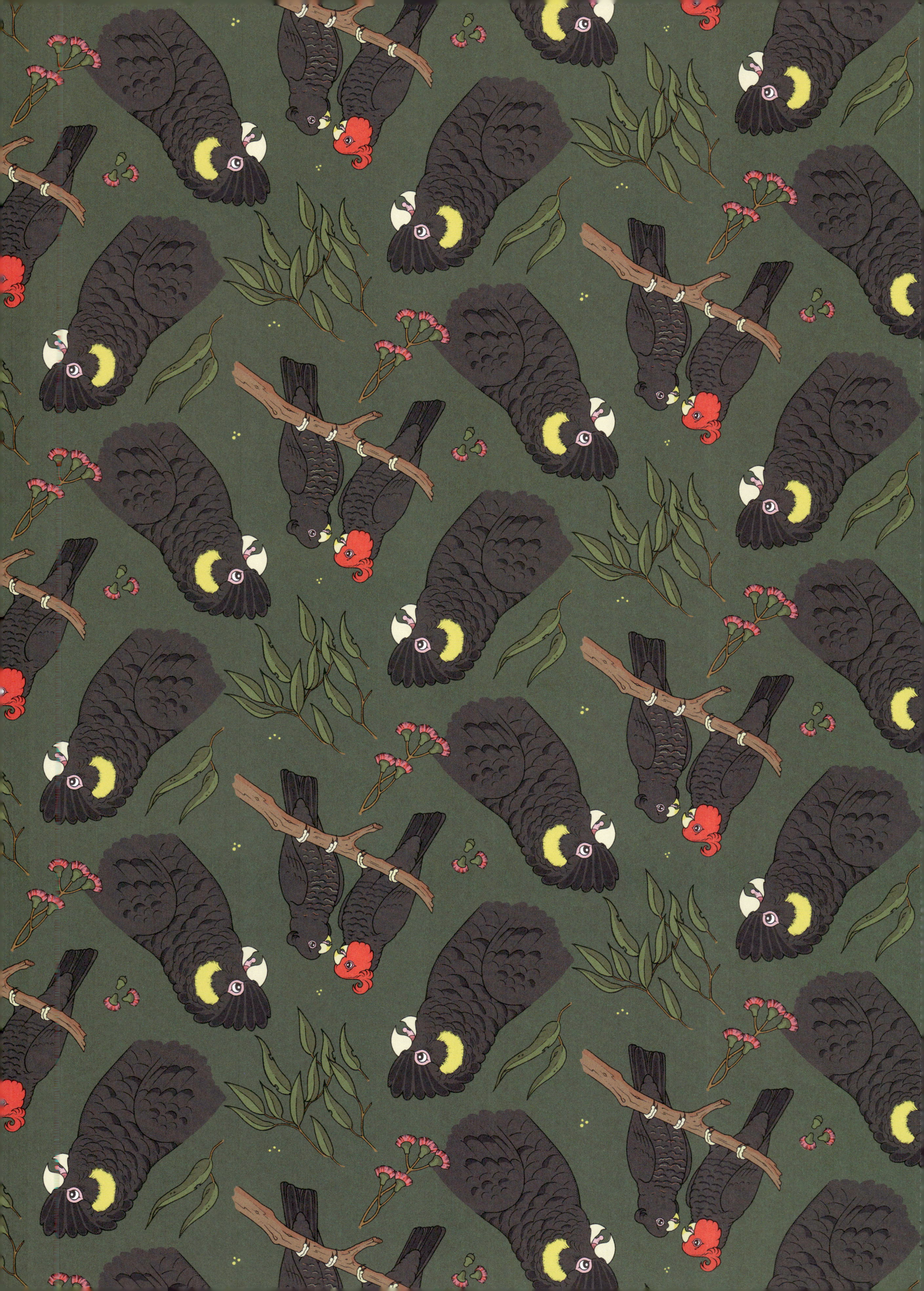

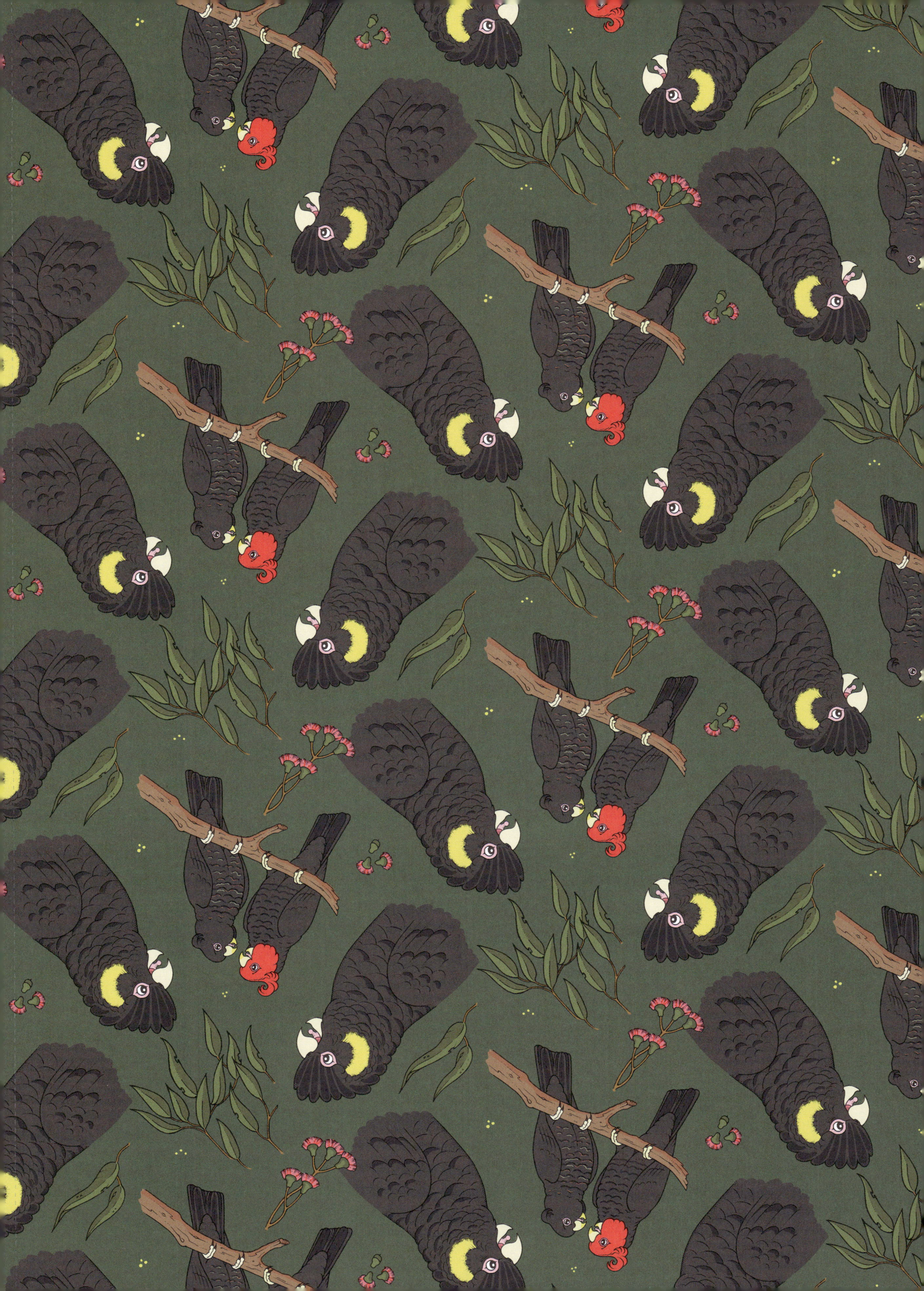

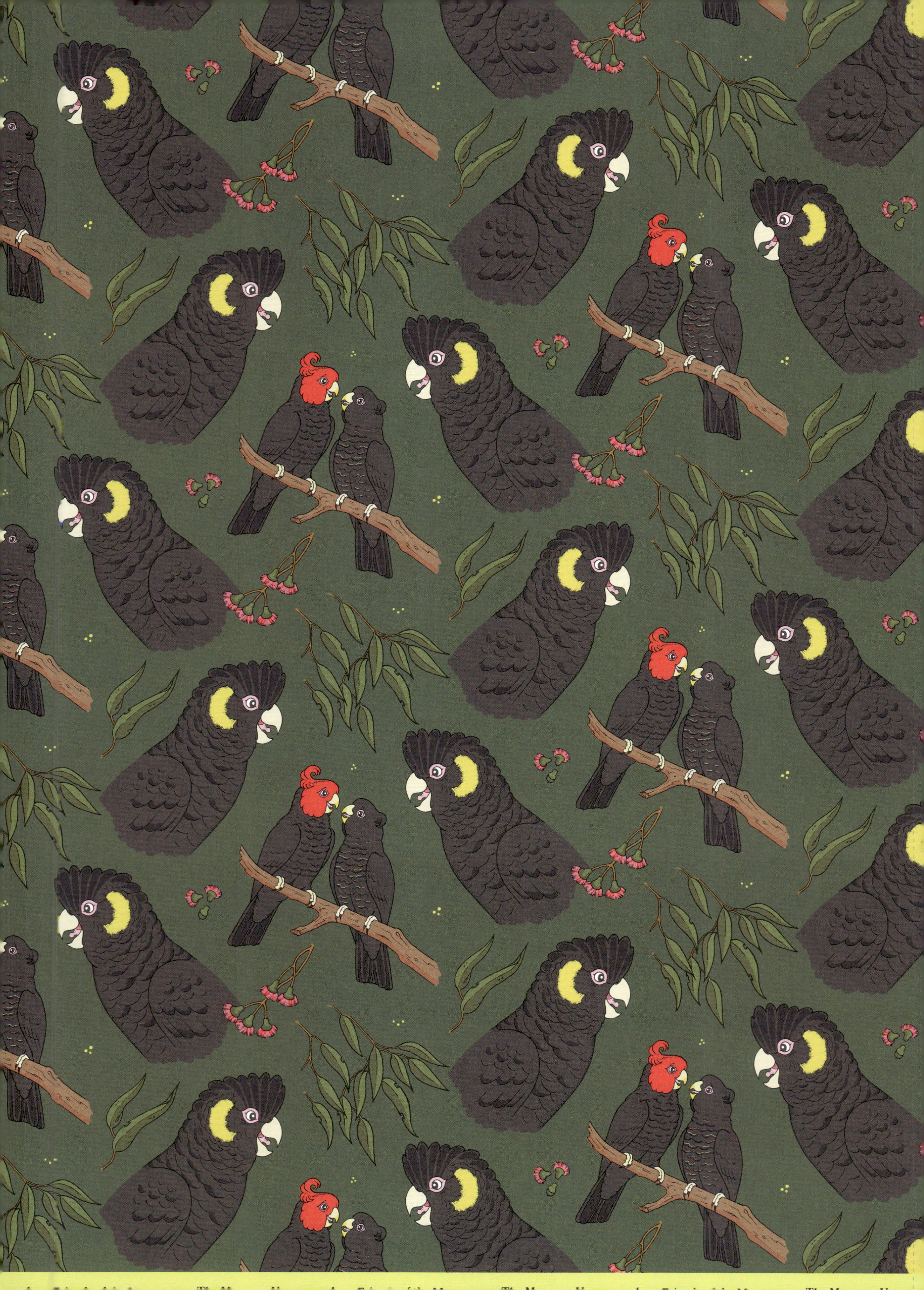

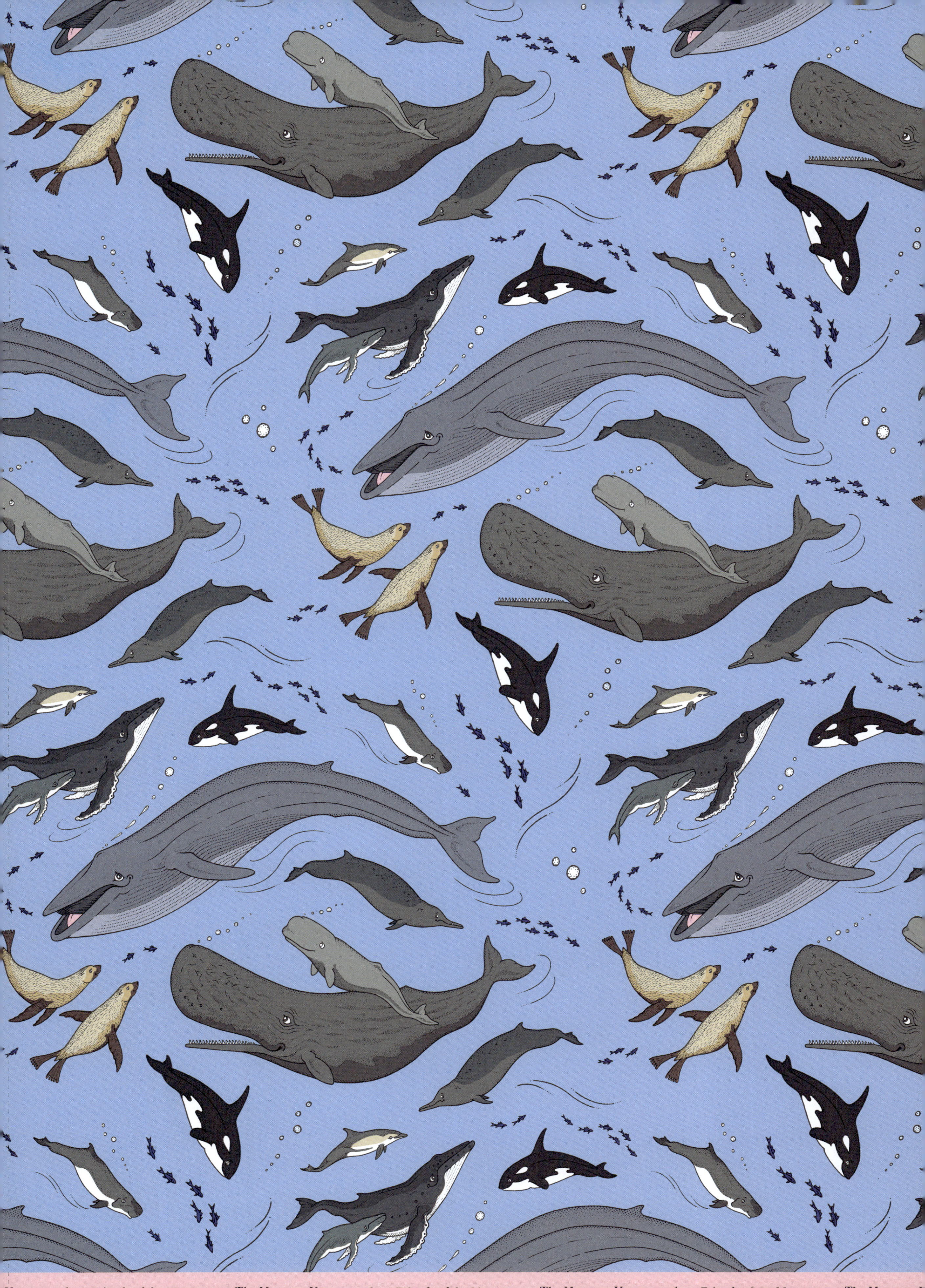

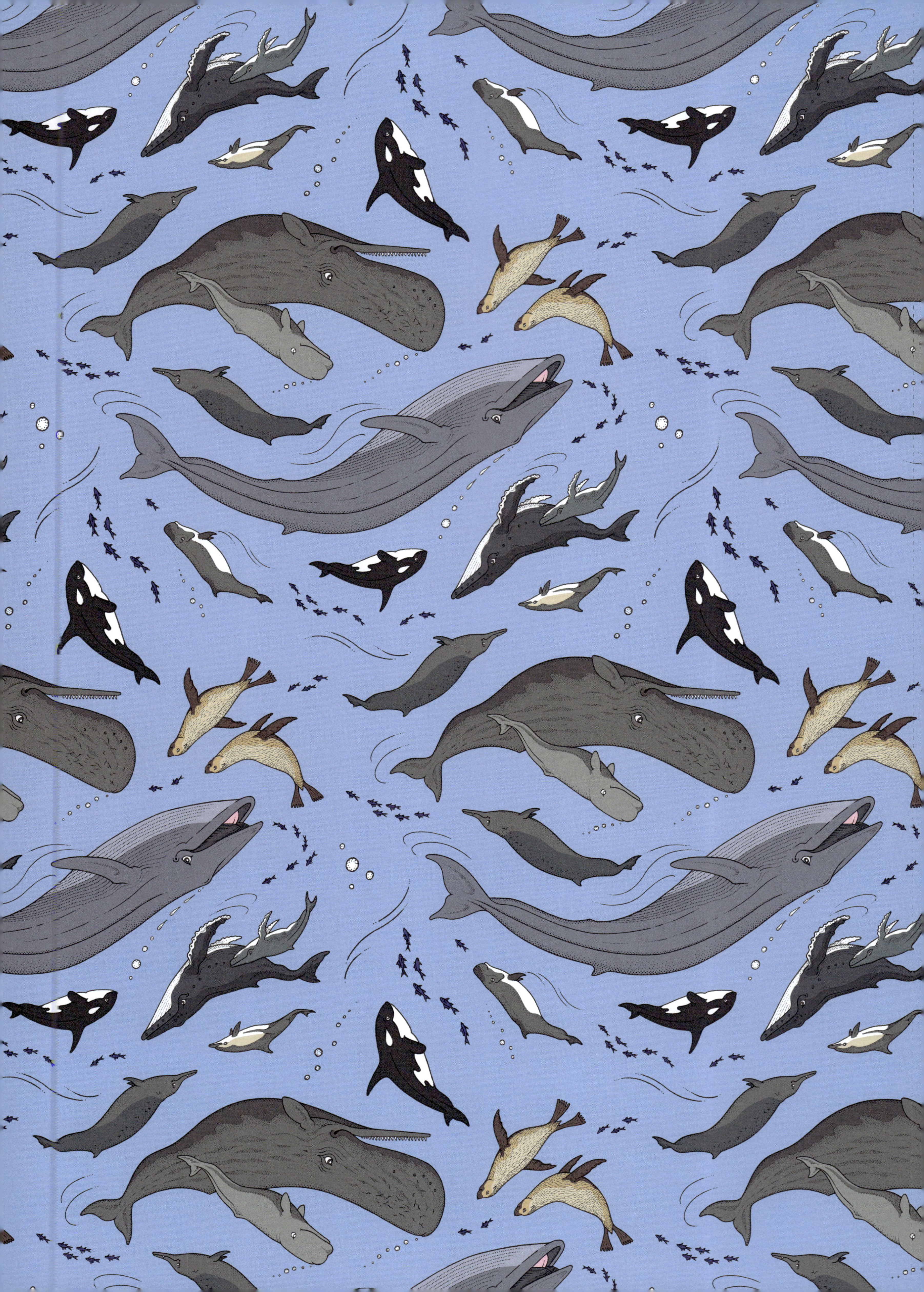

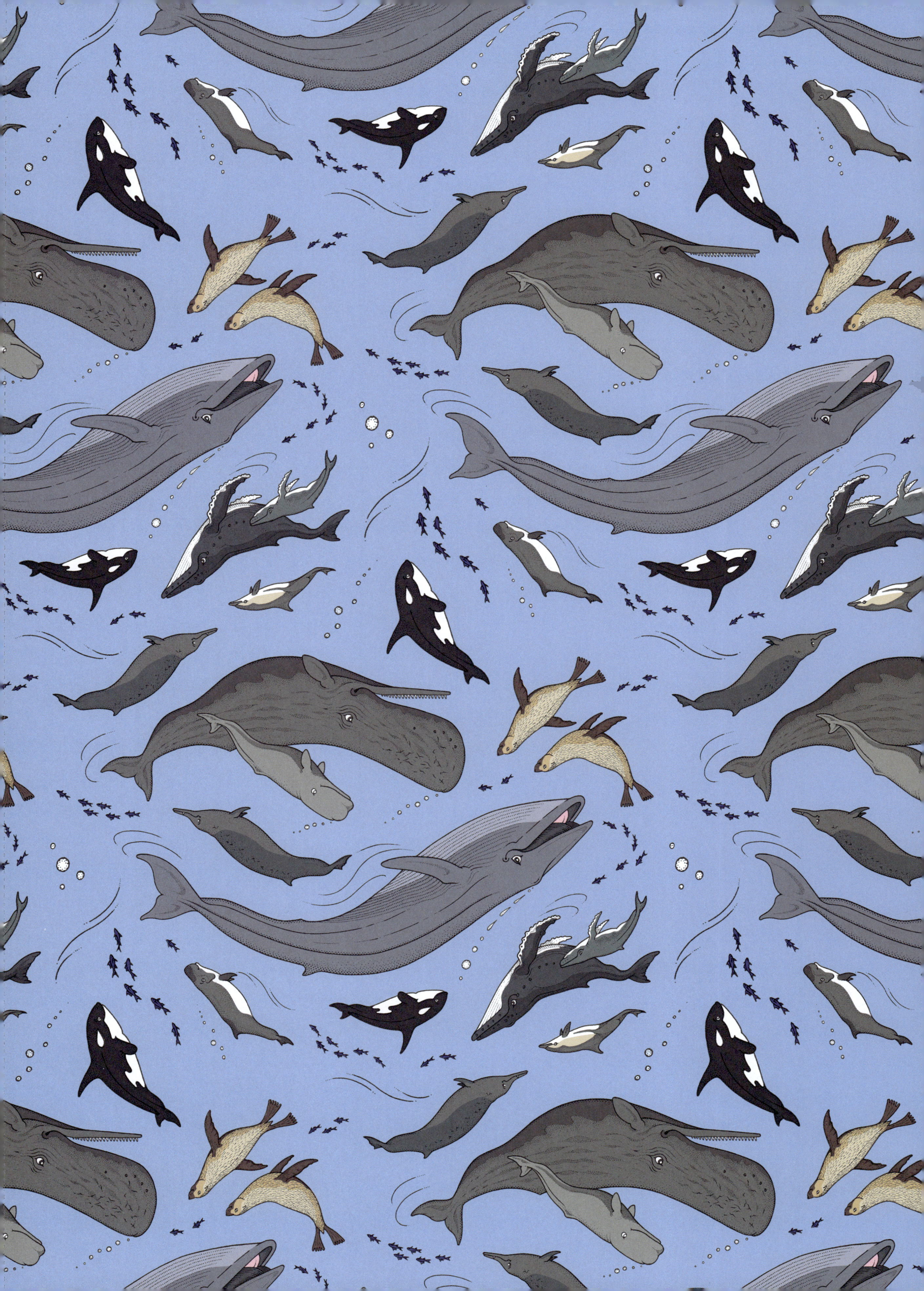

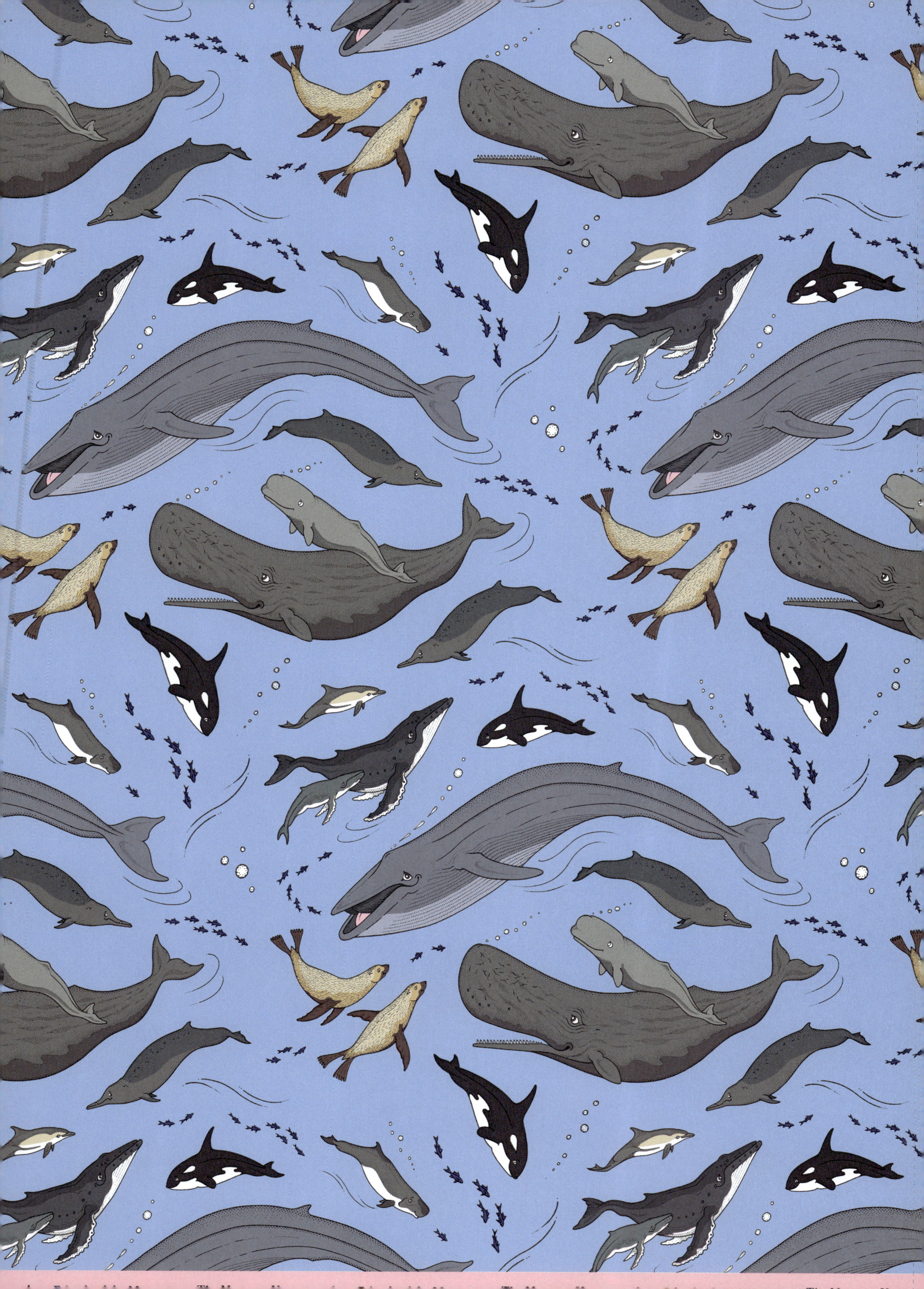

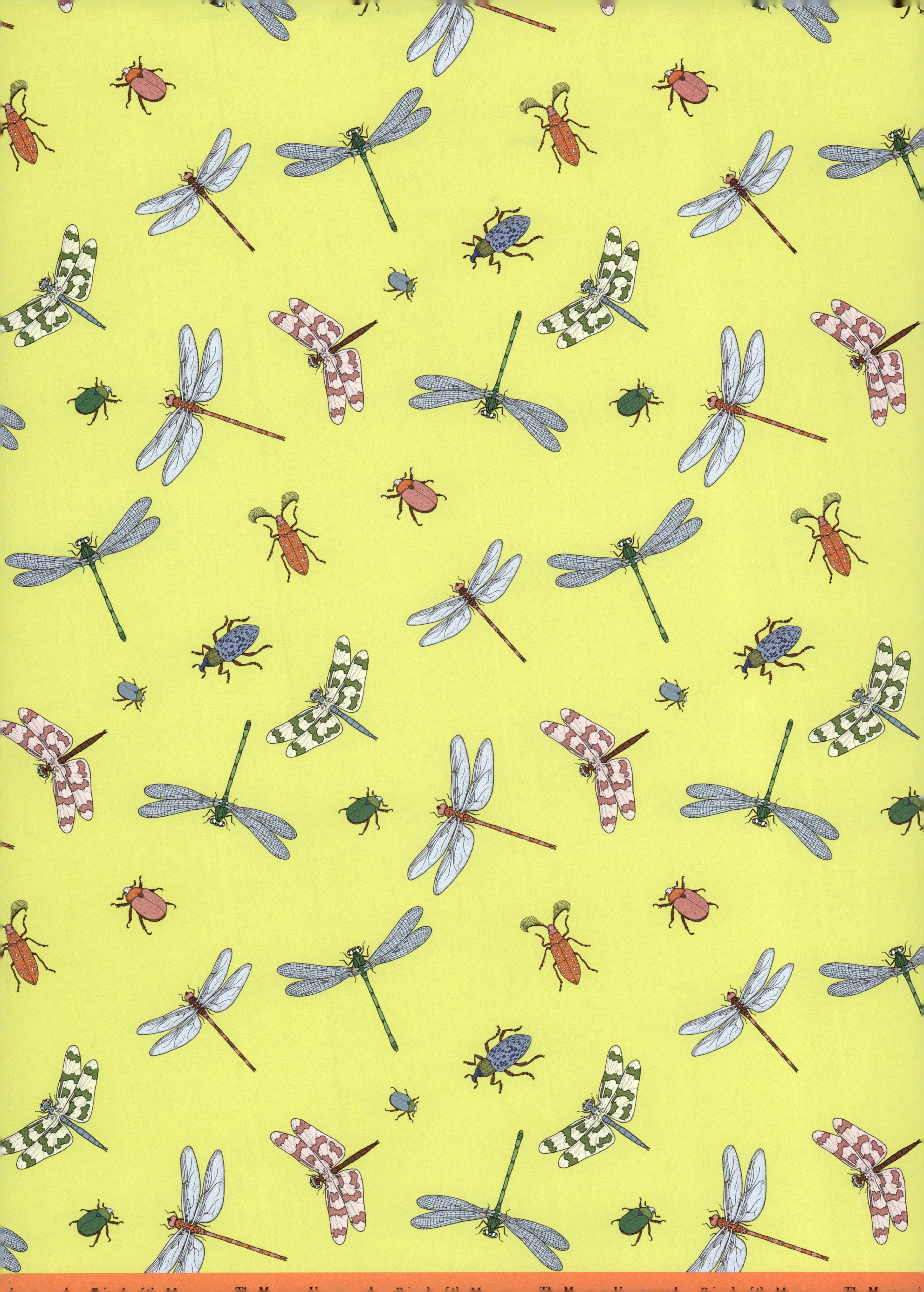

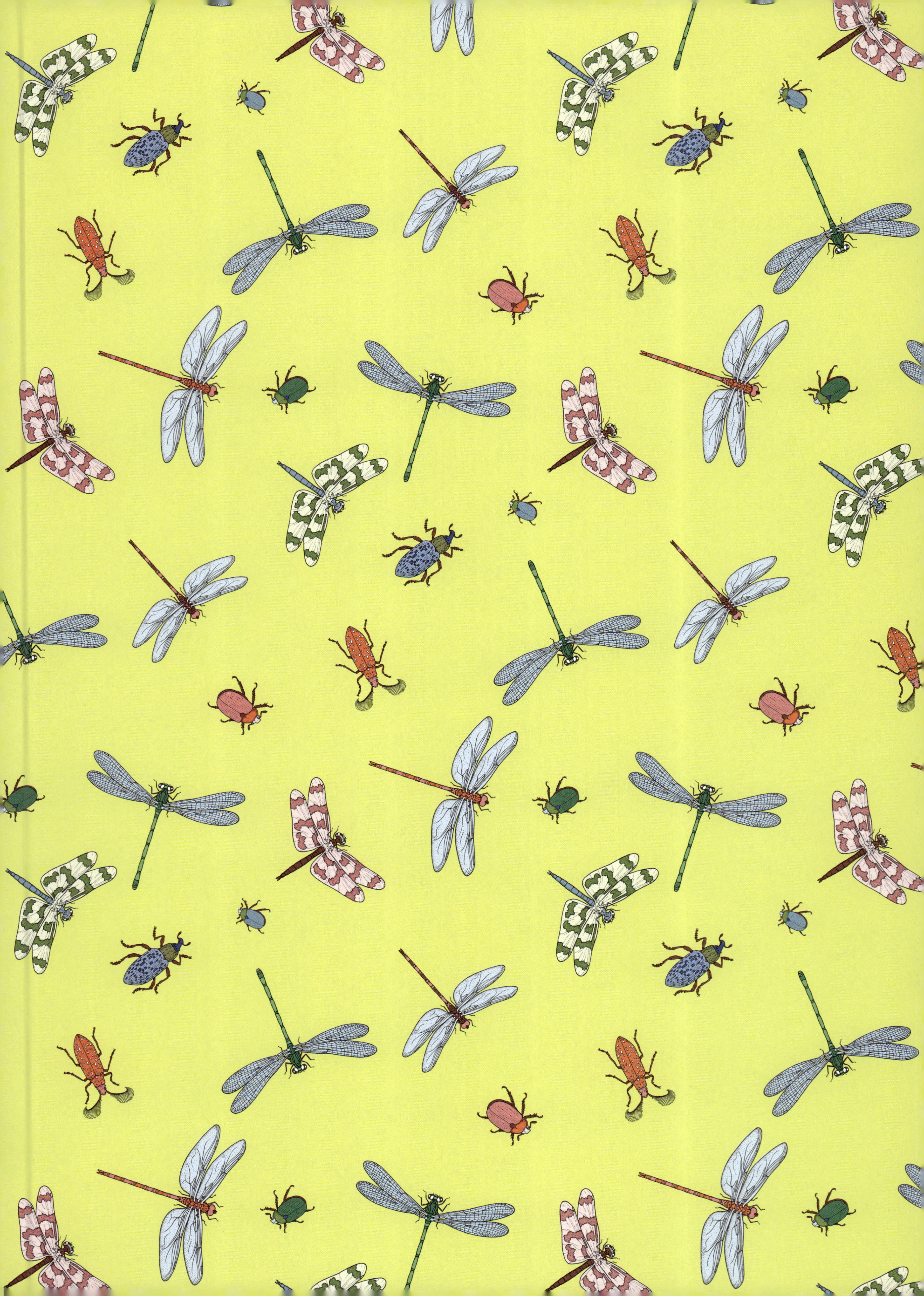

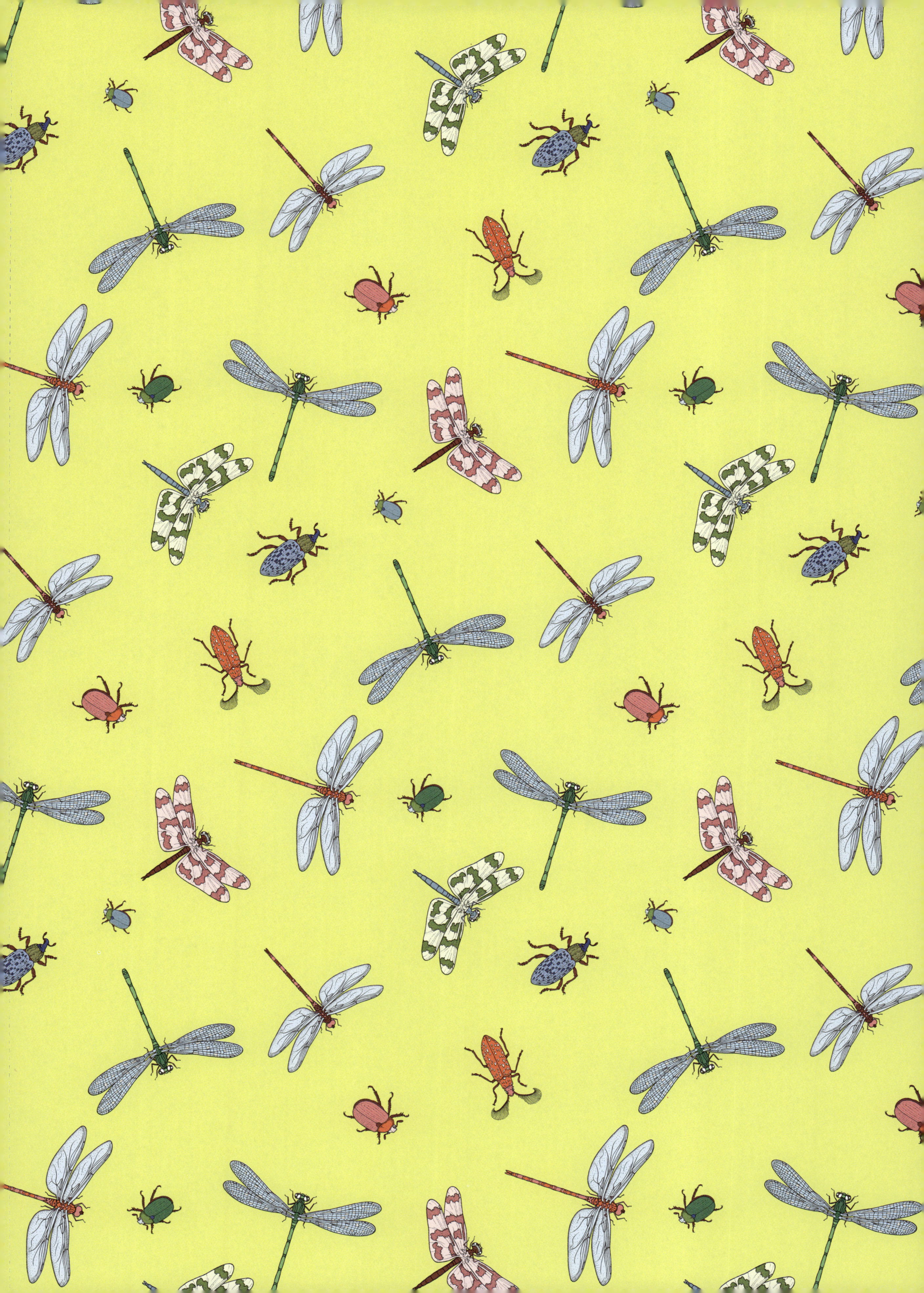

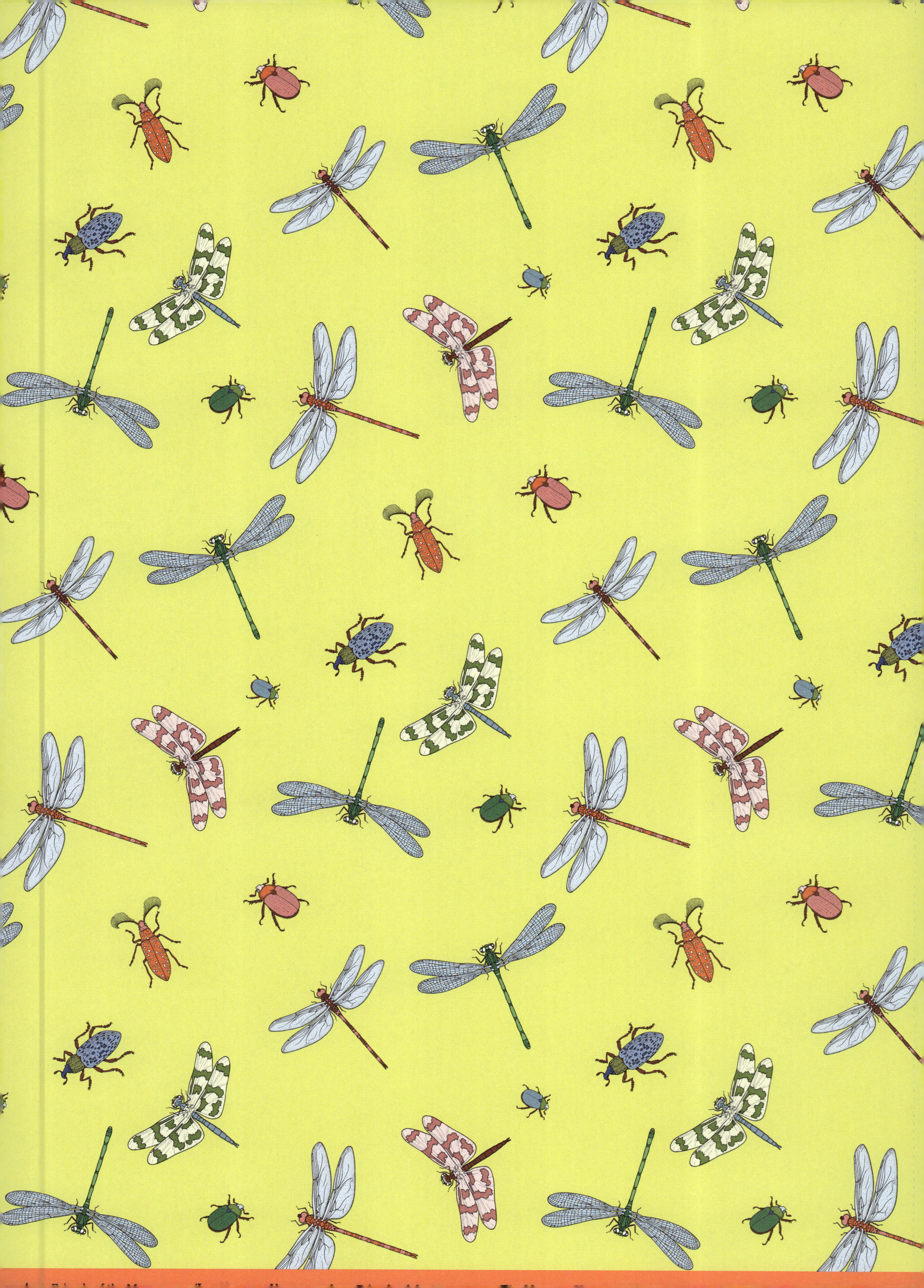

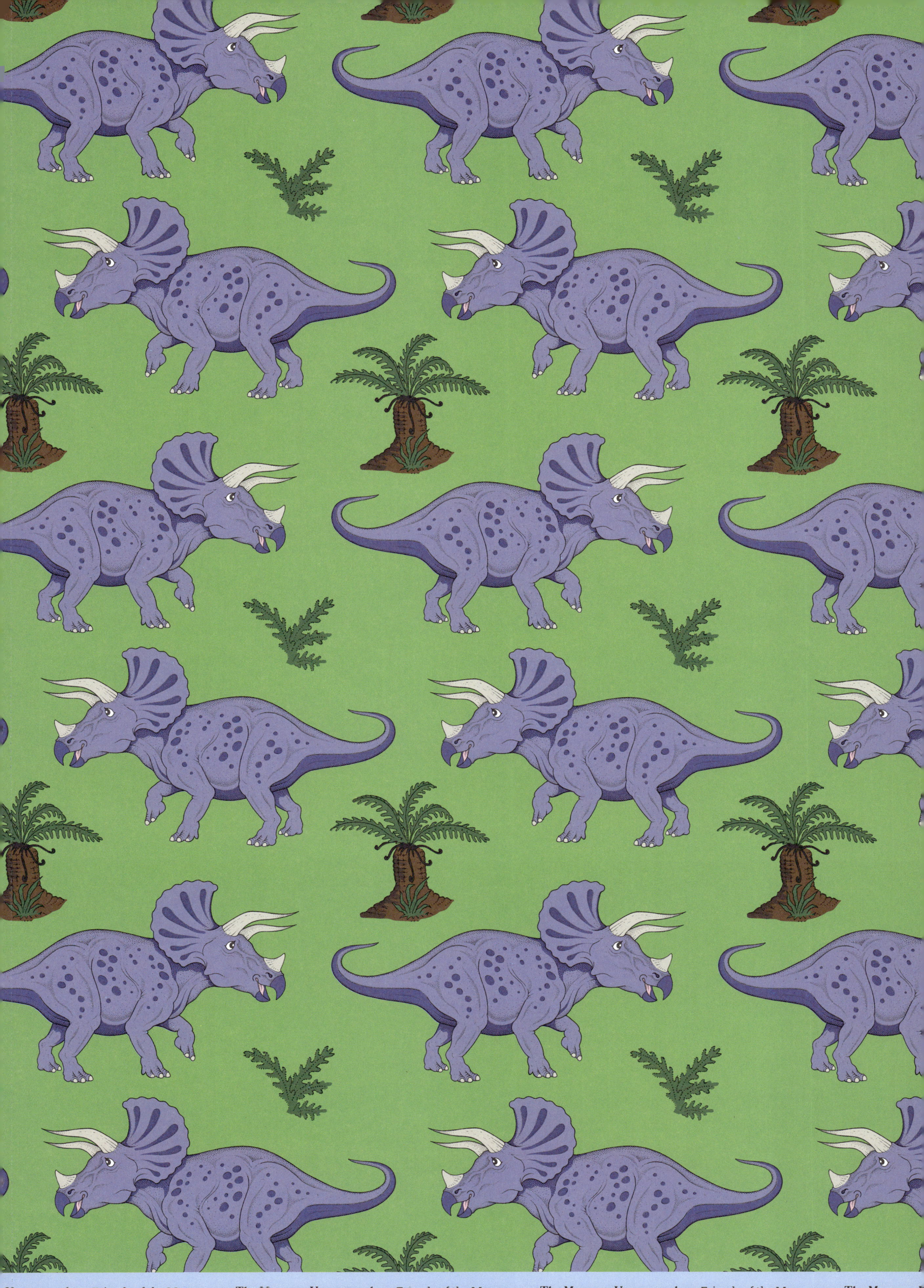

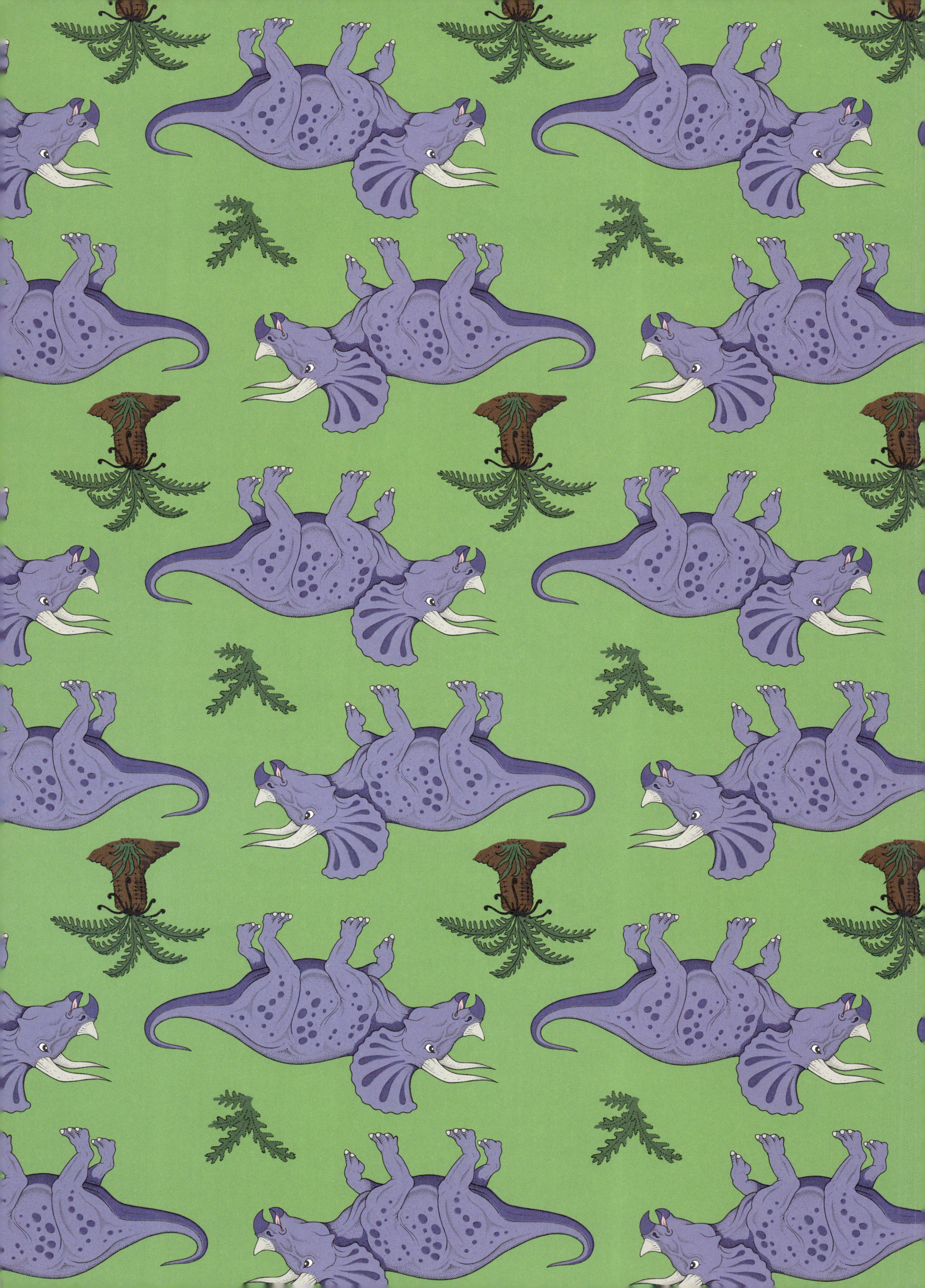

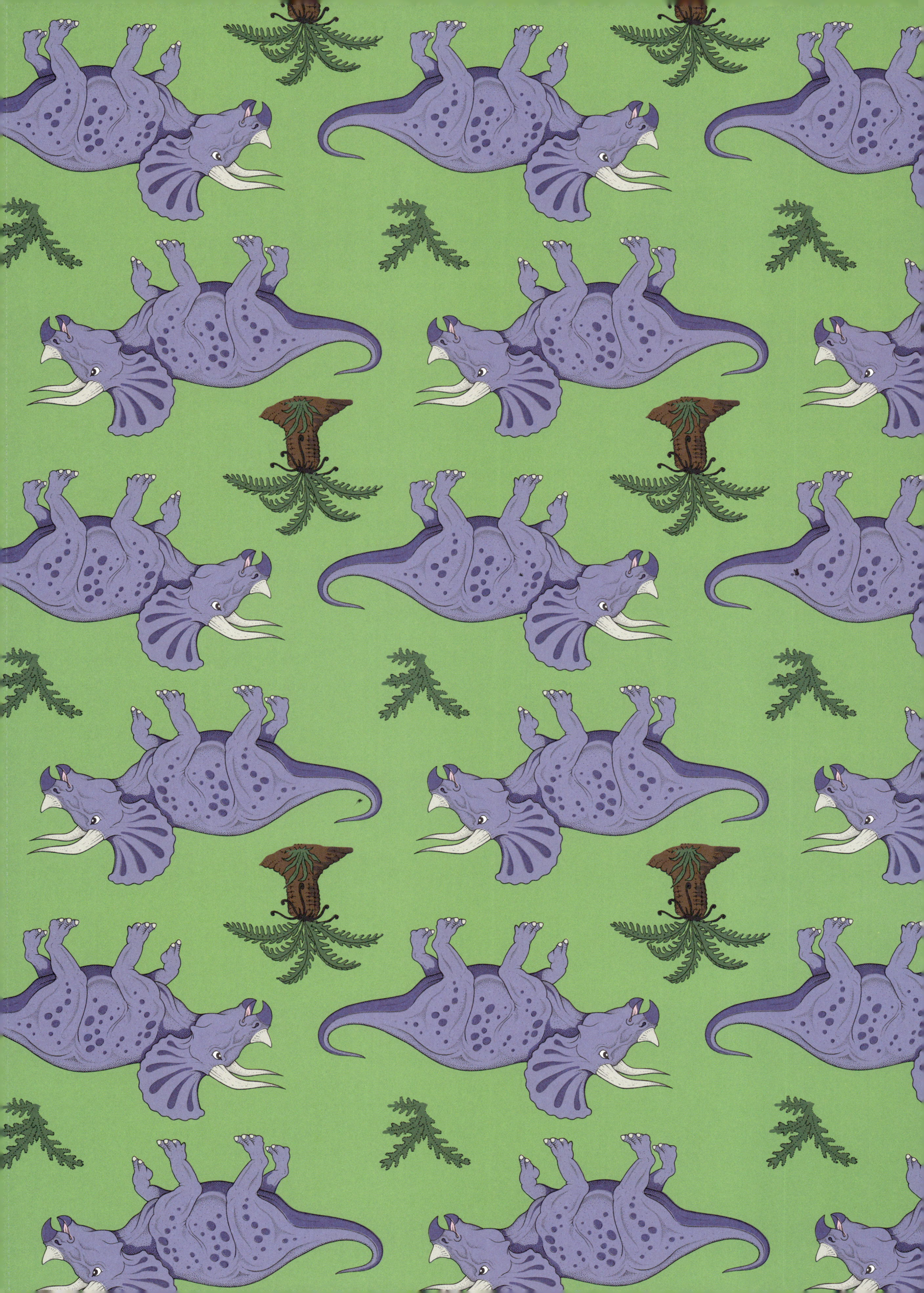

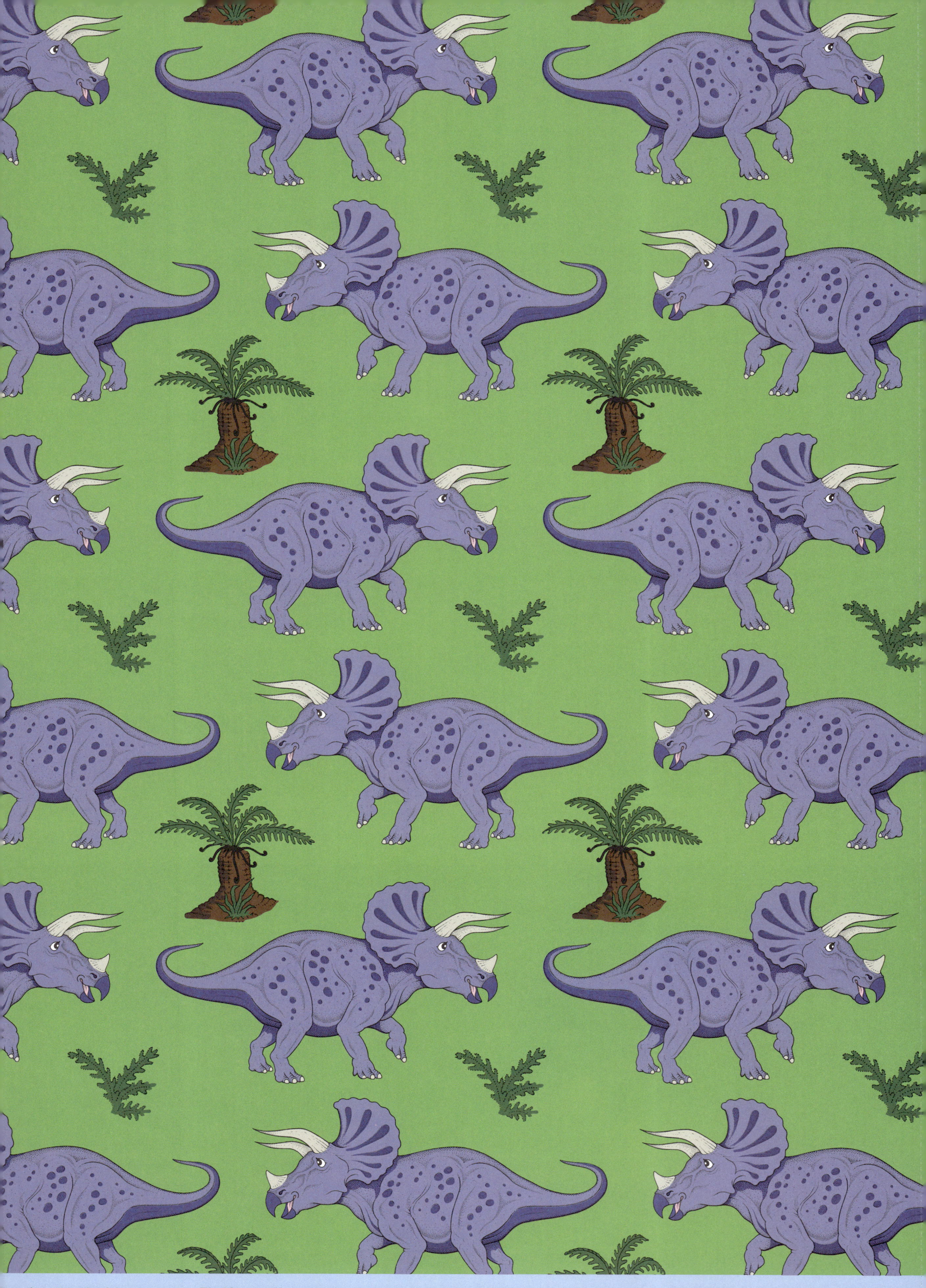

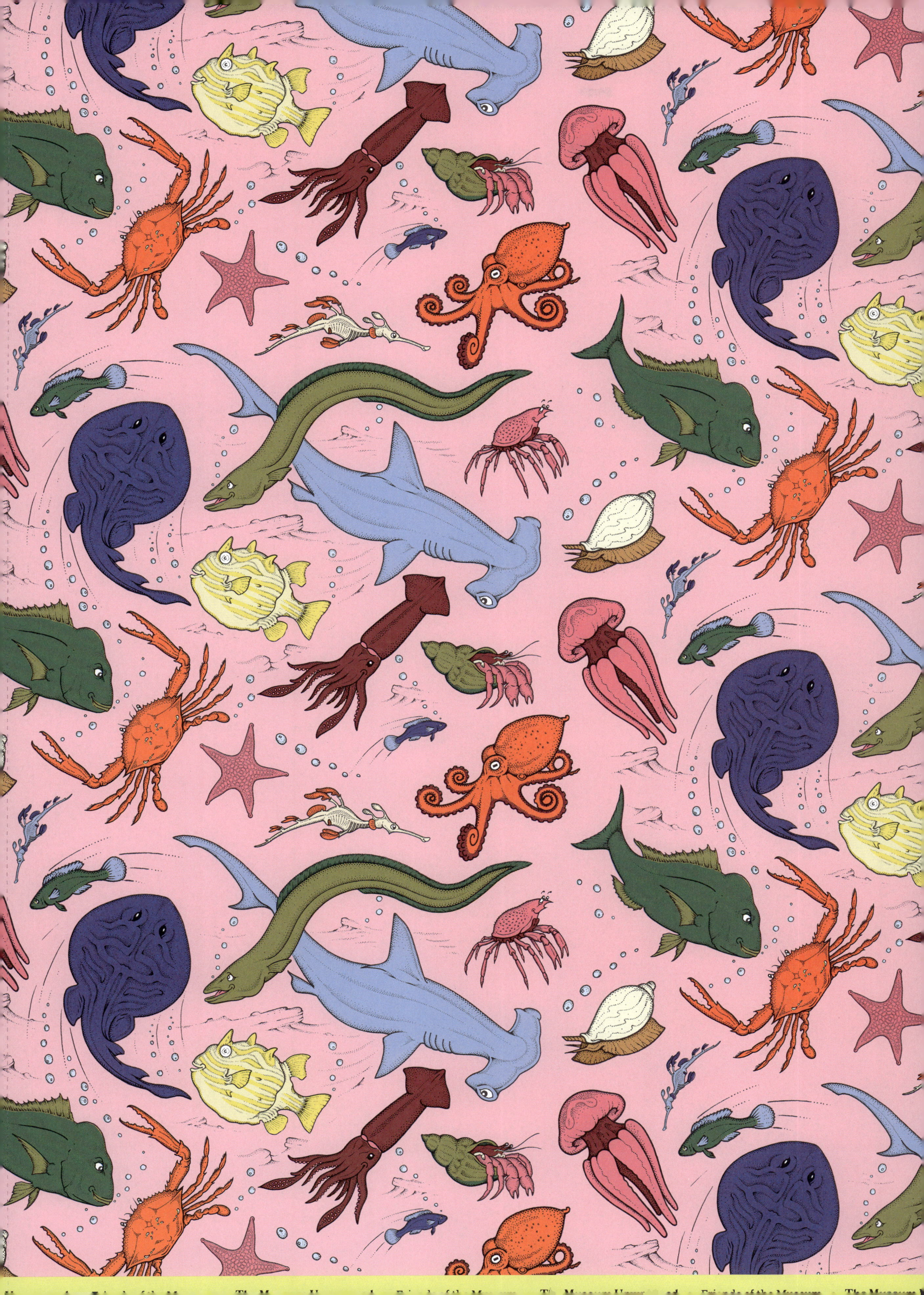

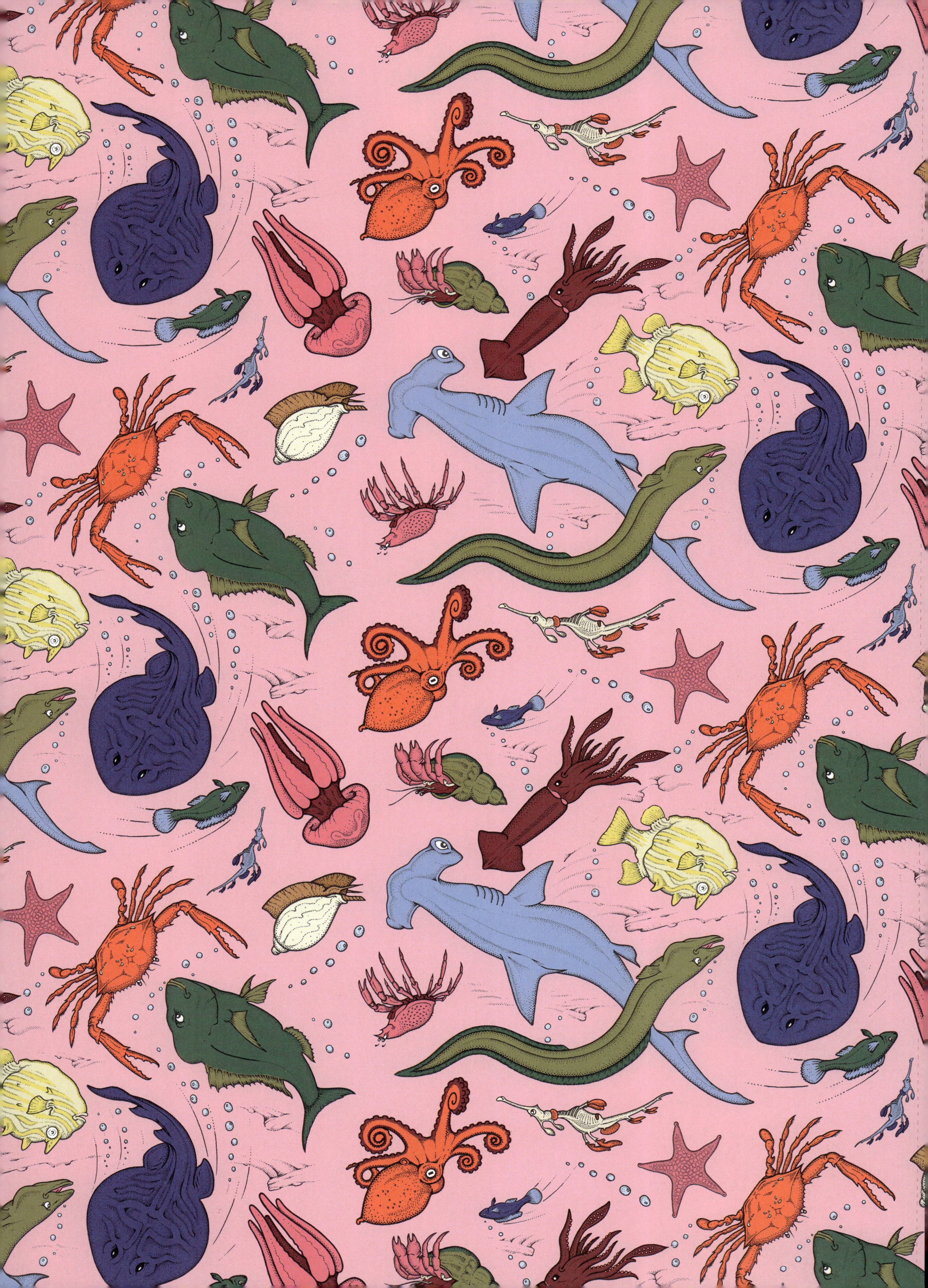

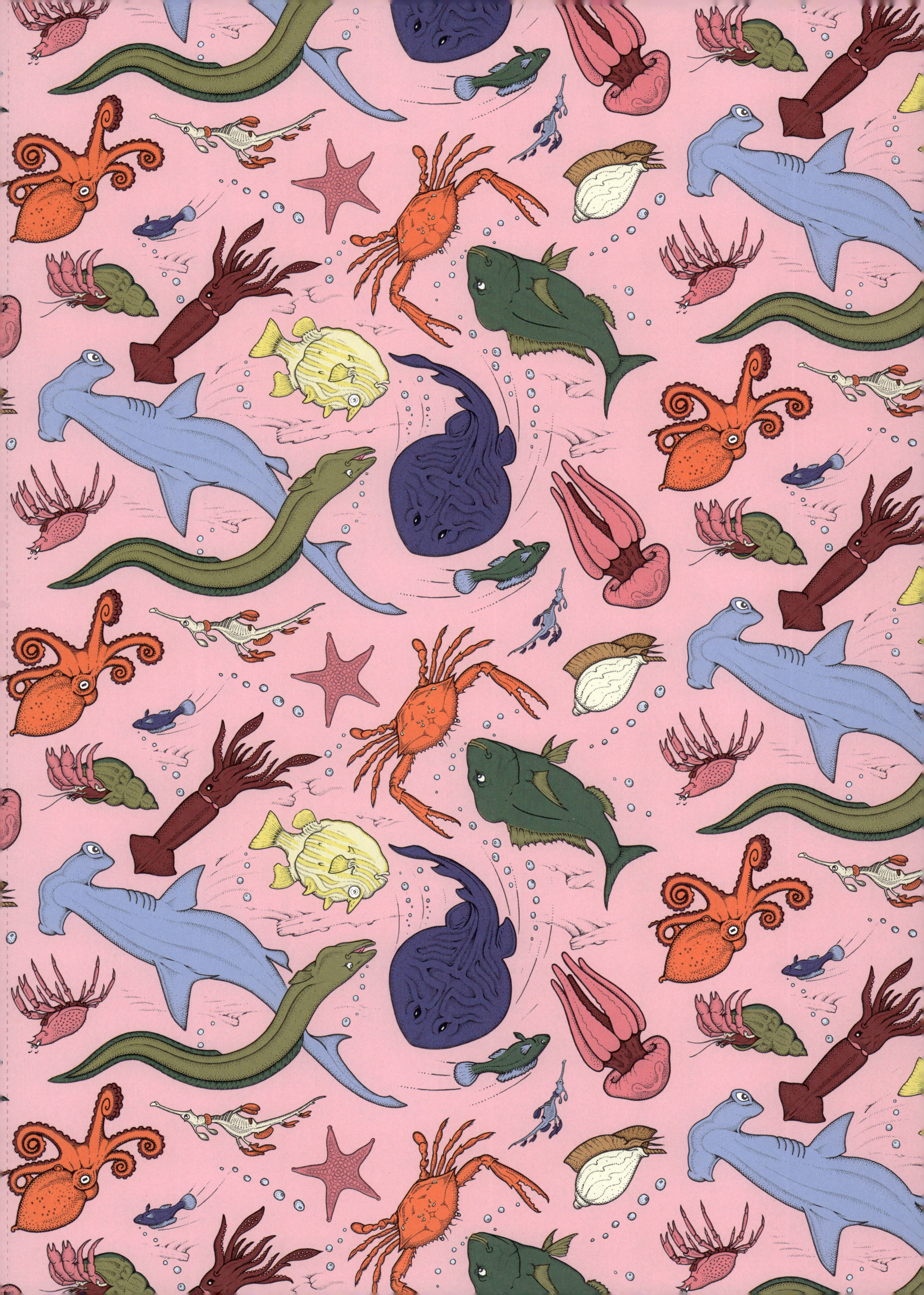

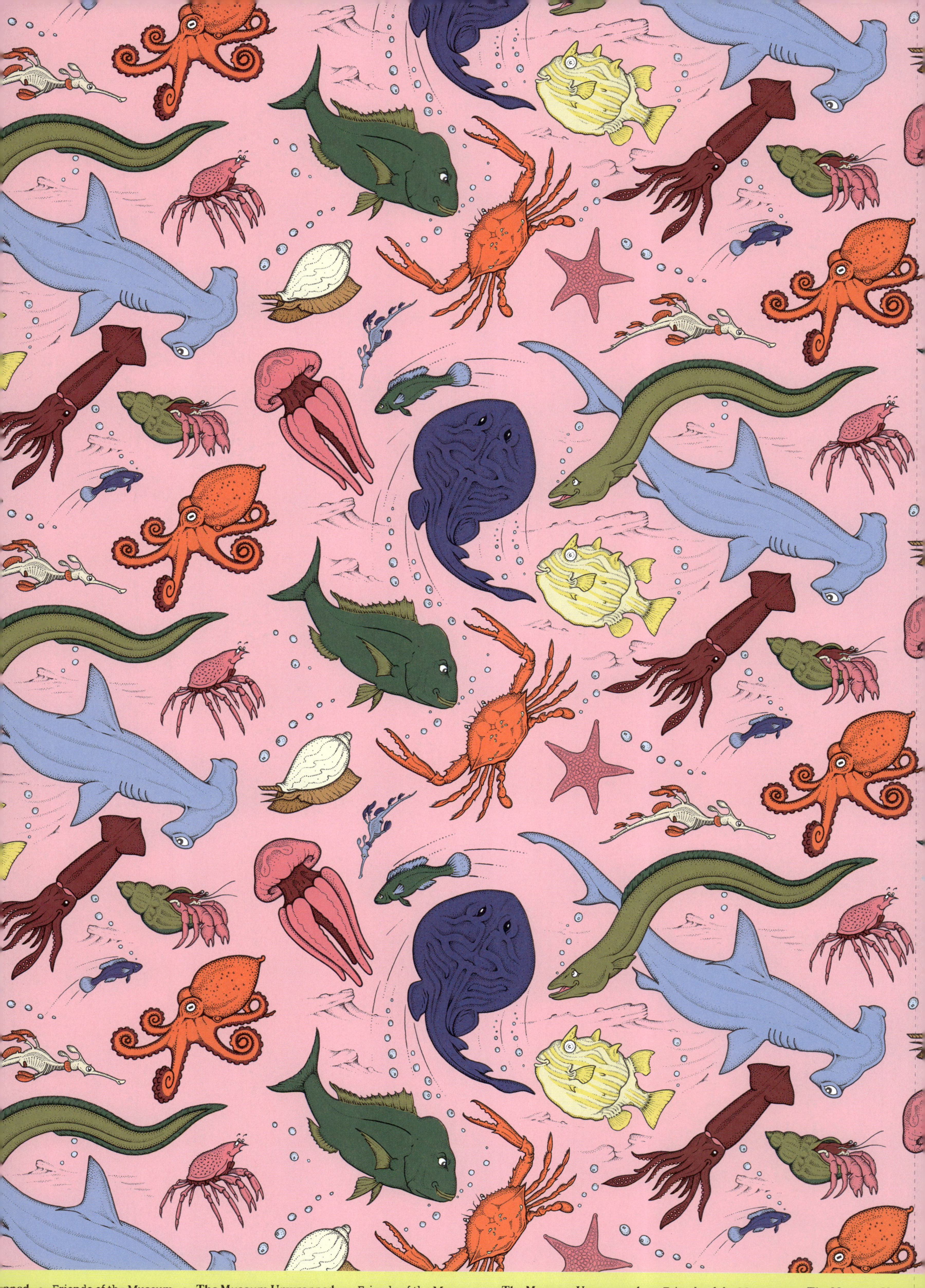
Friends of the Museum • The Museum Unwrapped

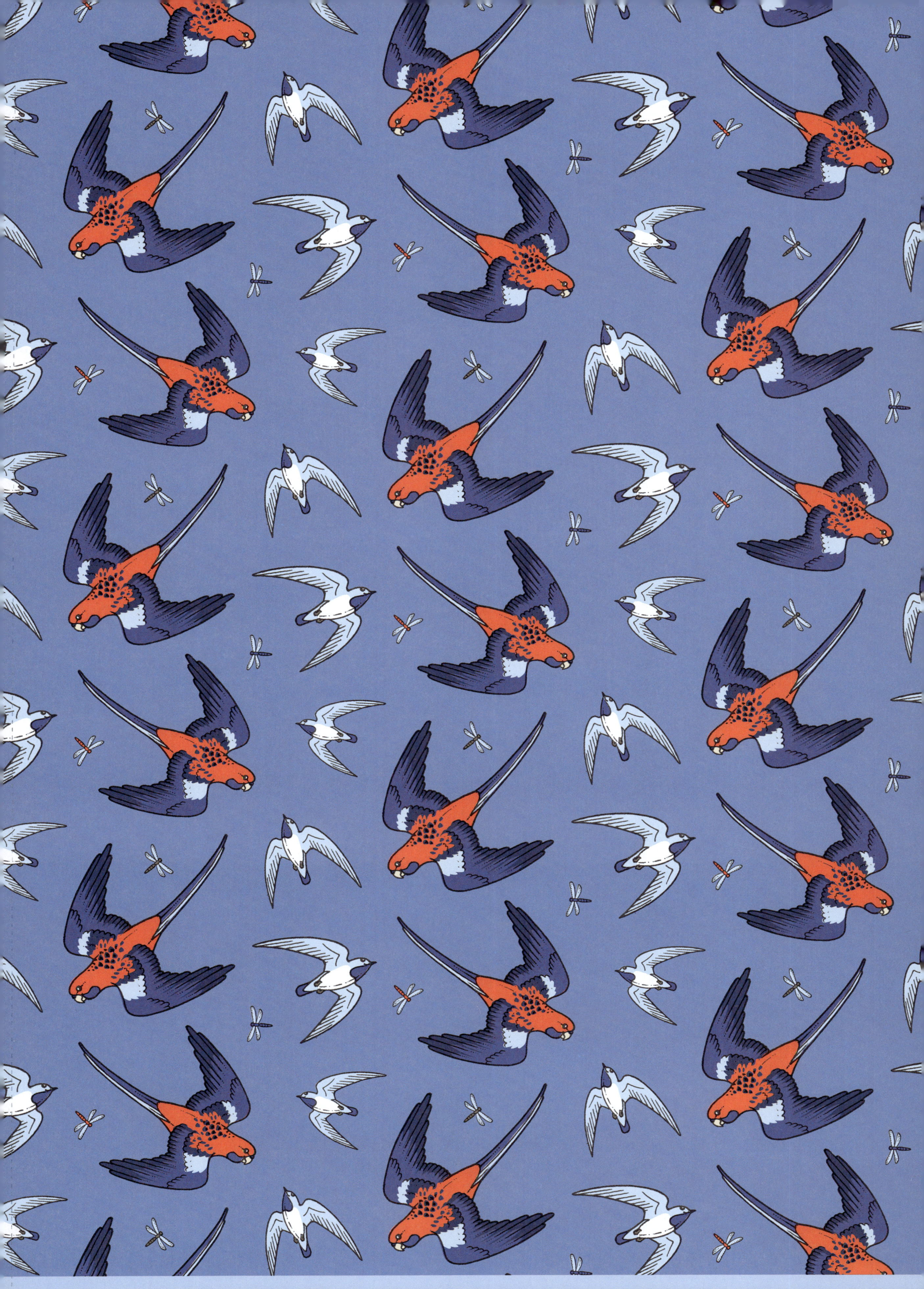

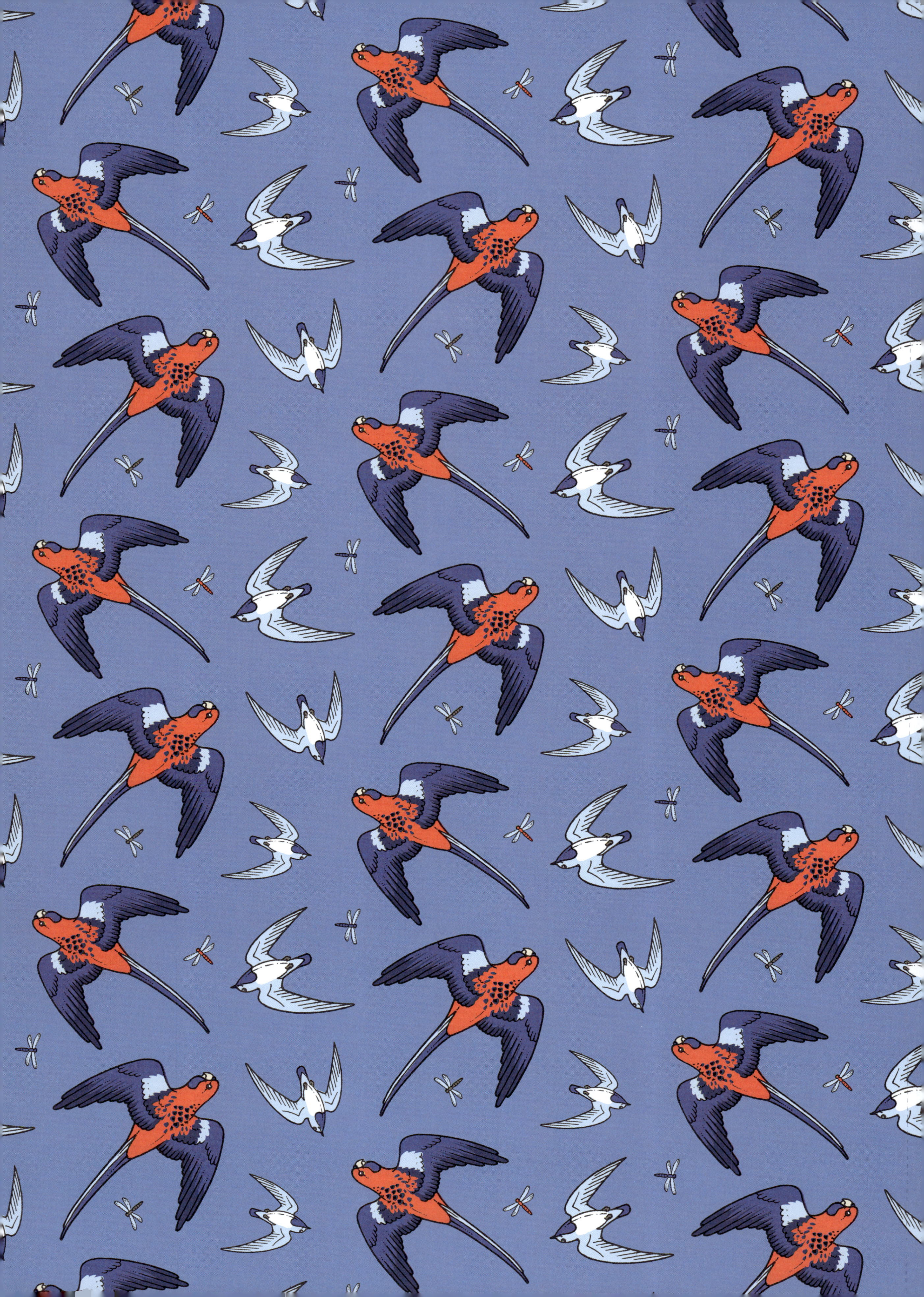

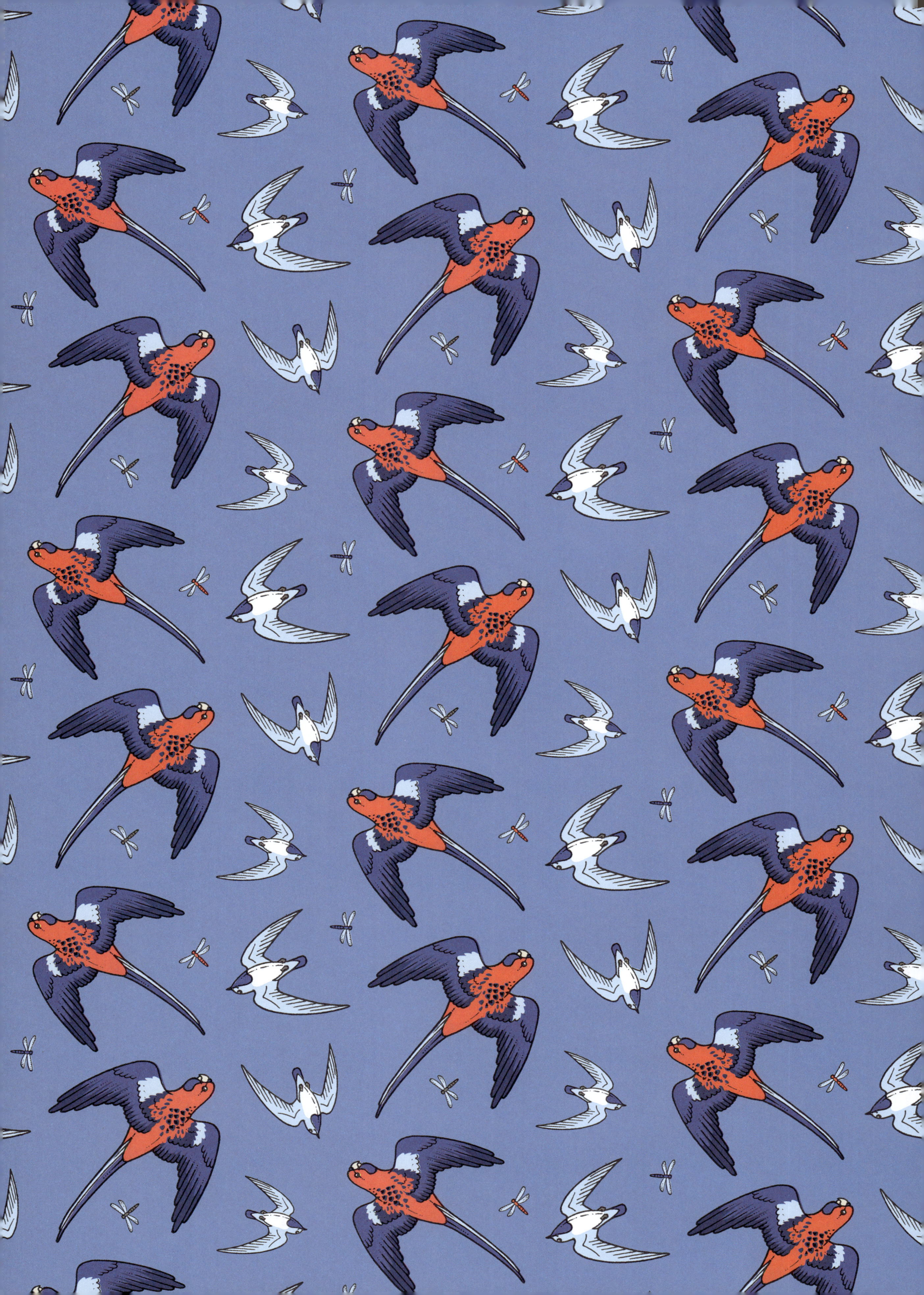

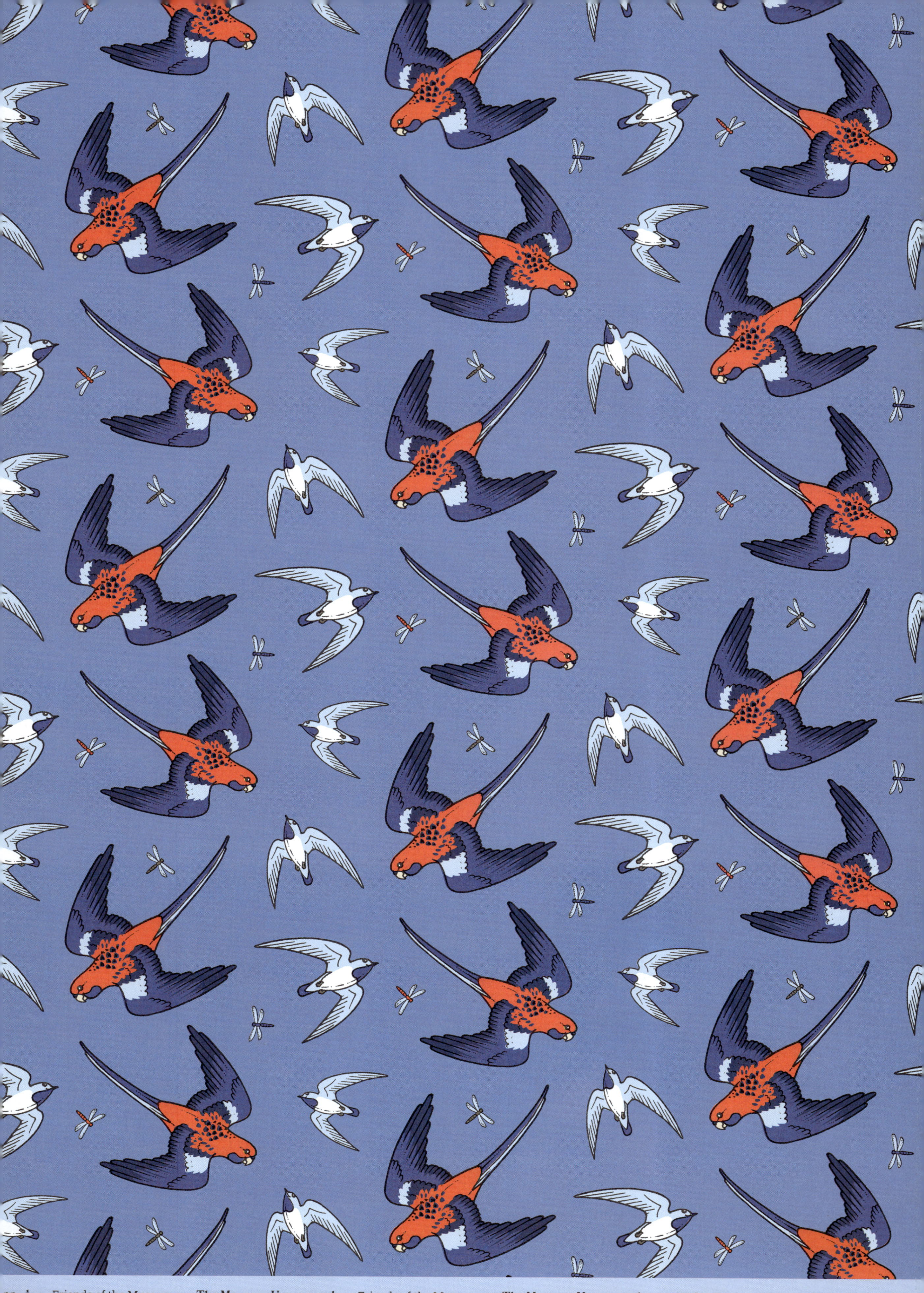

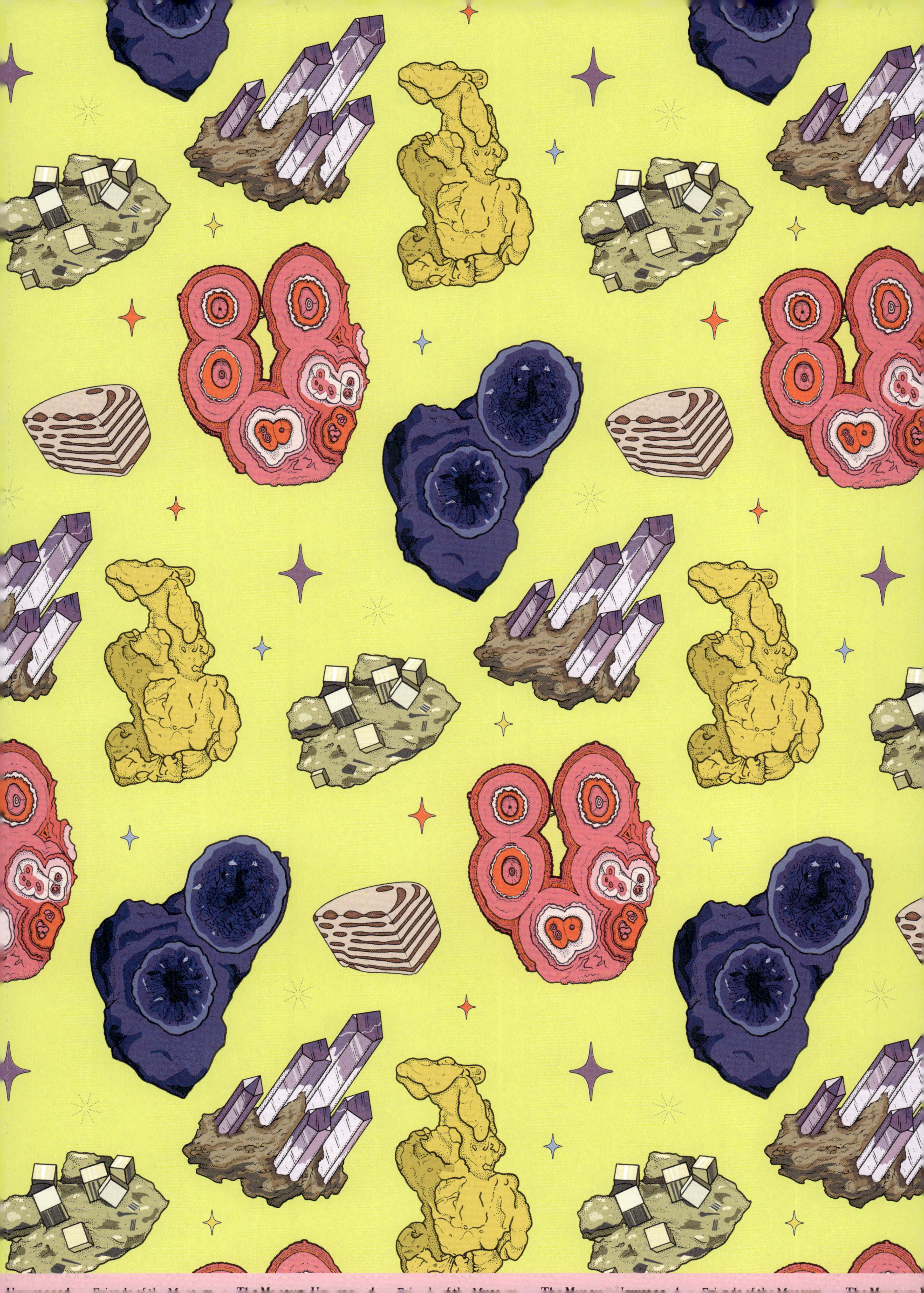

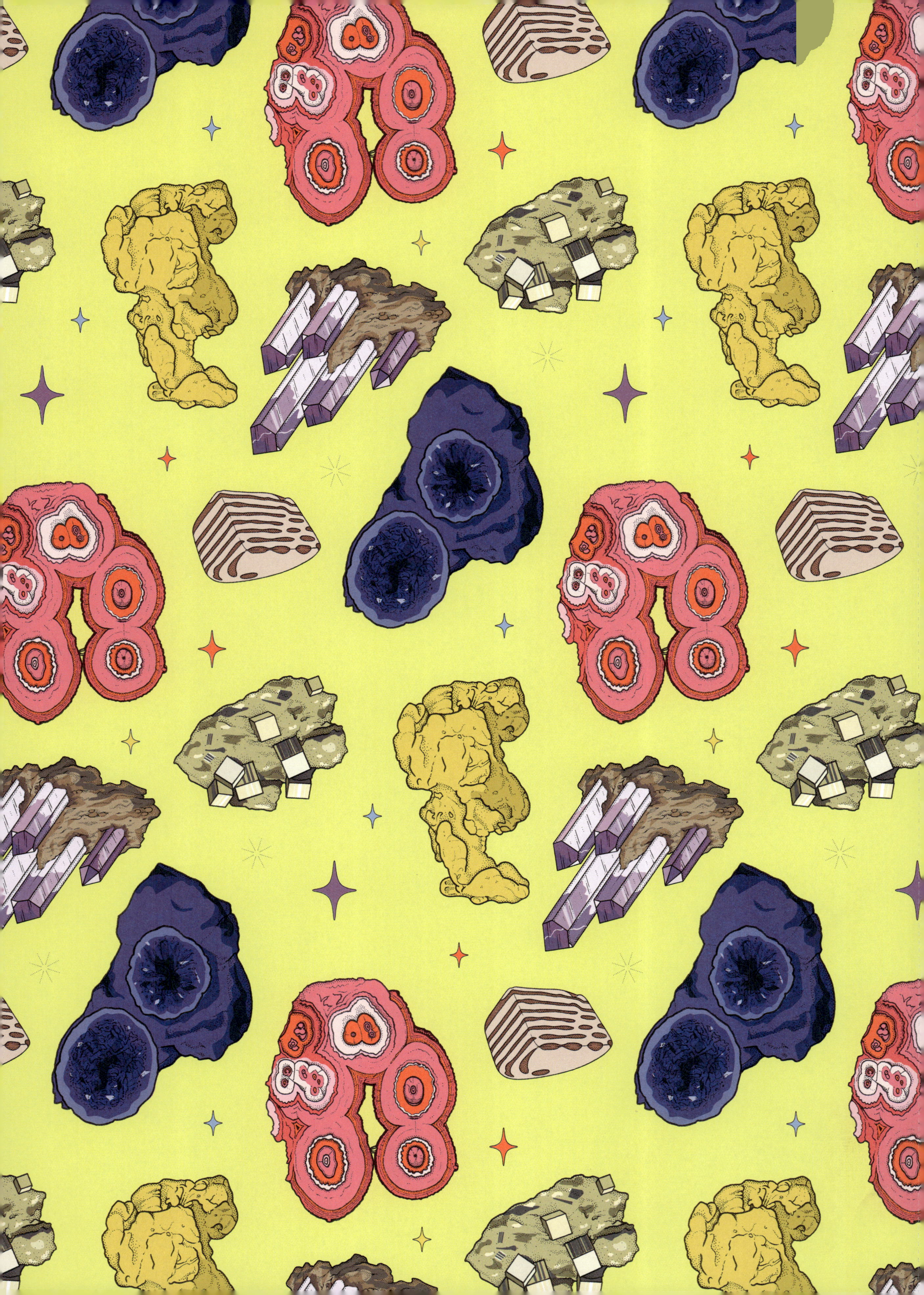

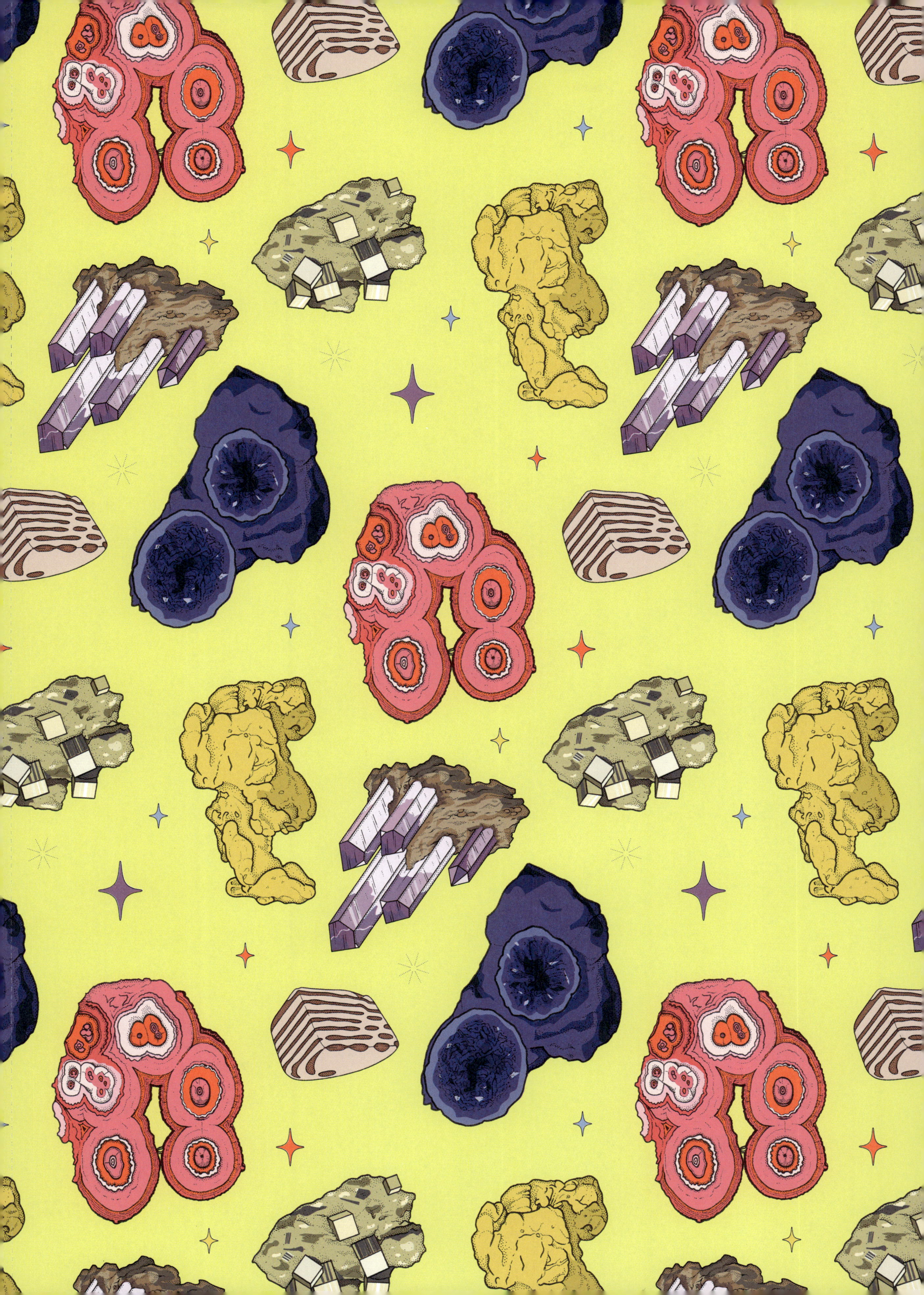

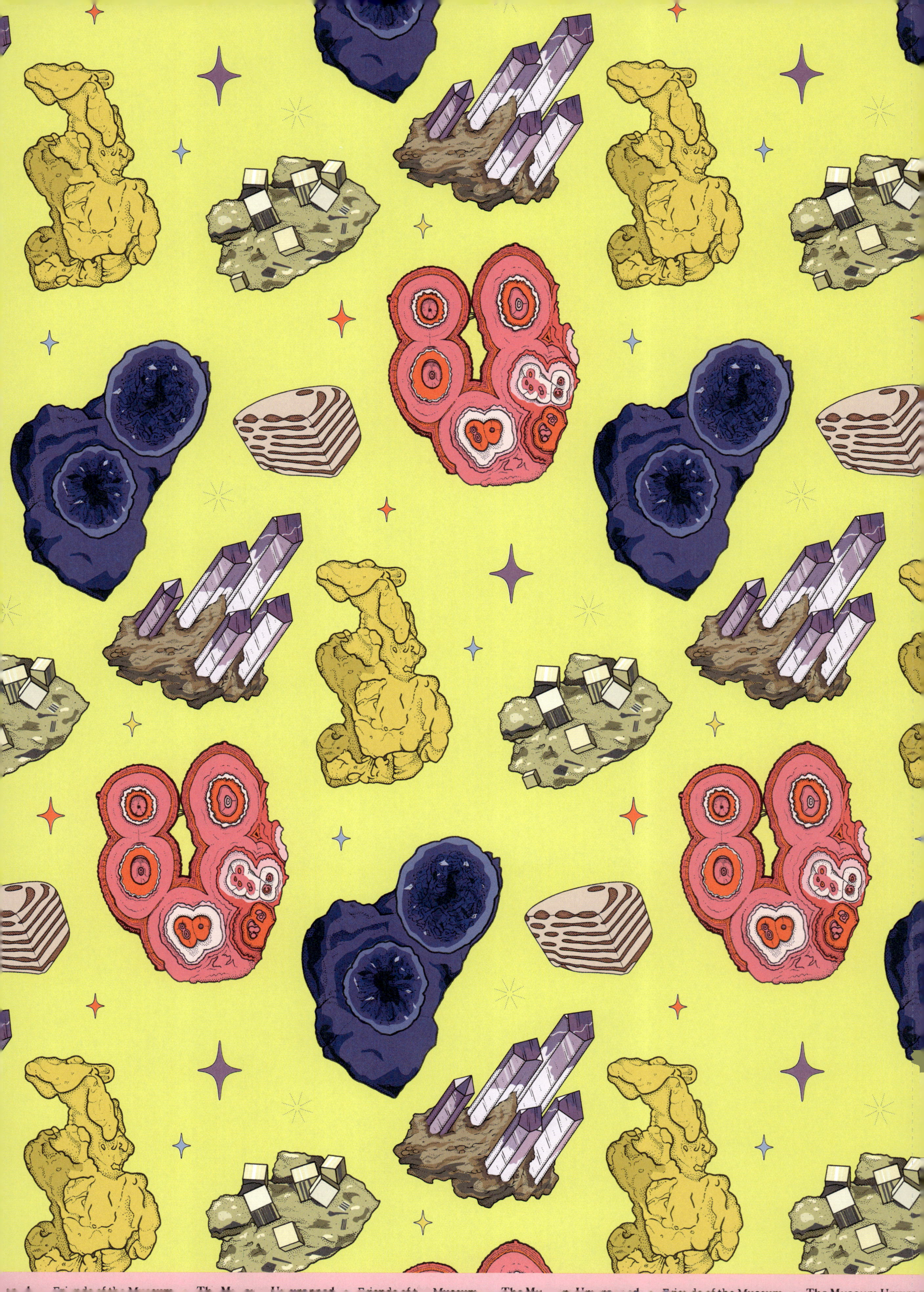

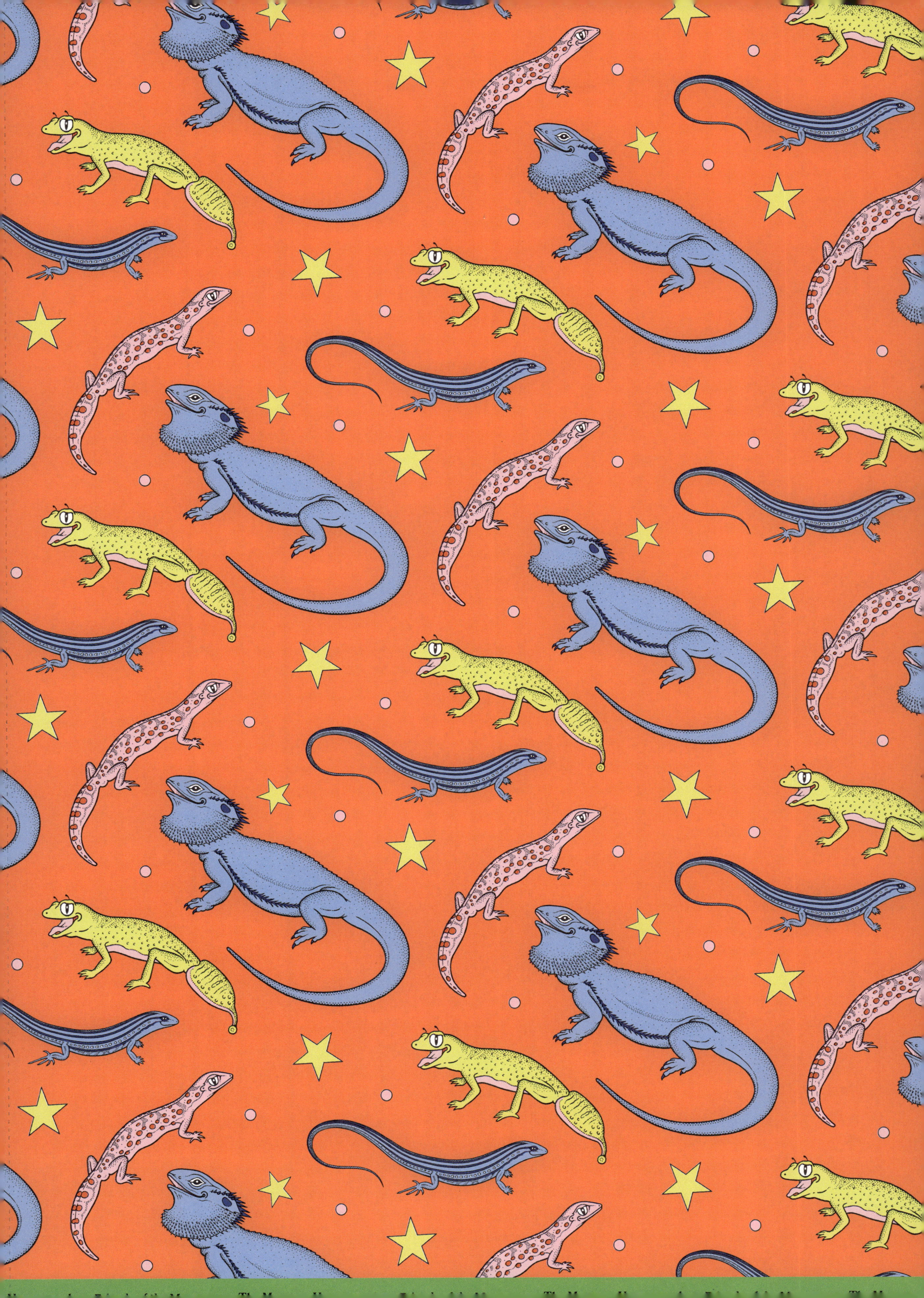

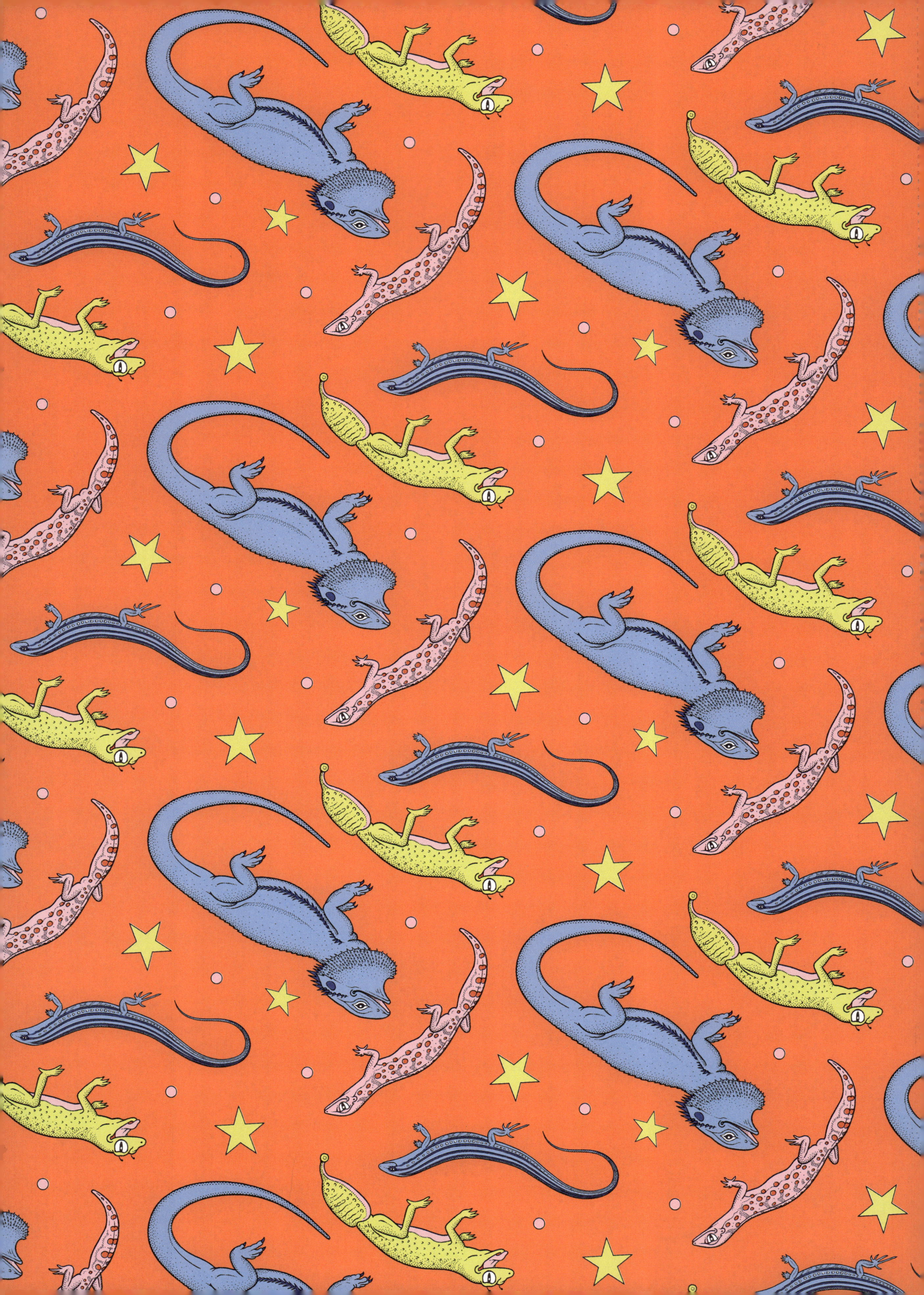

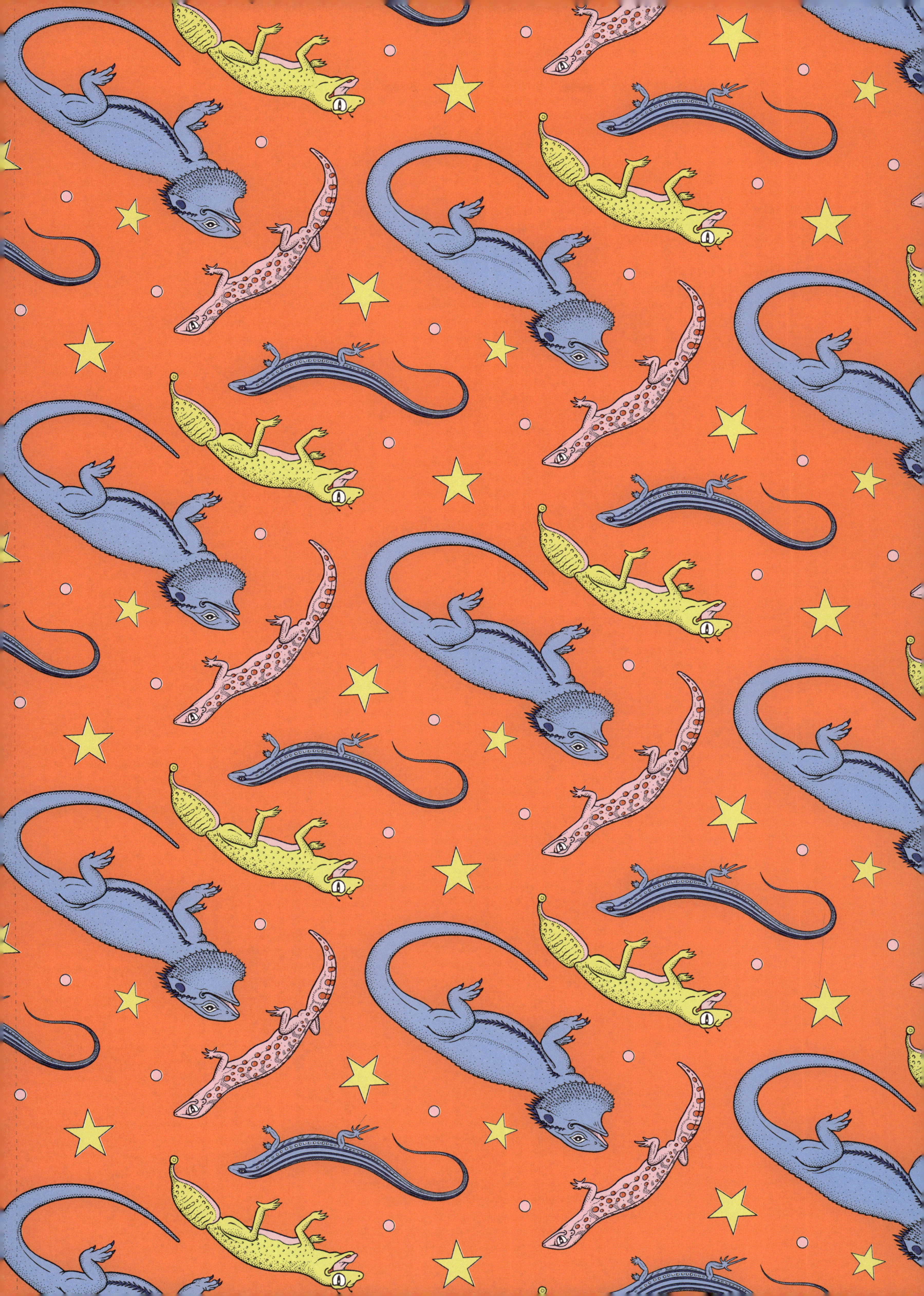

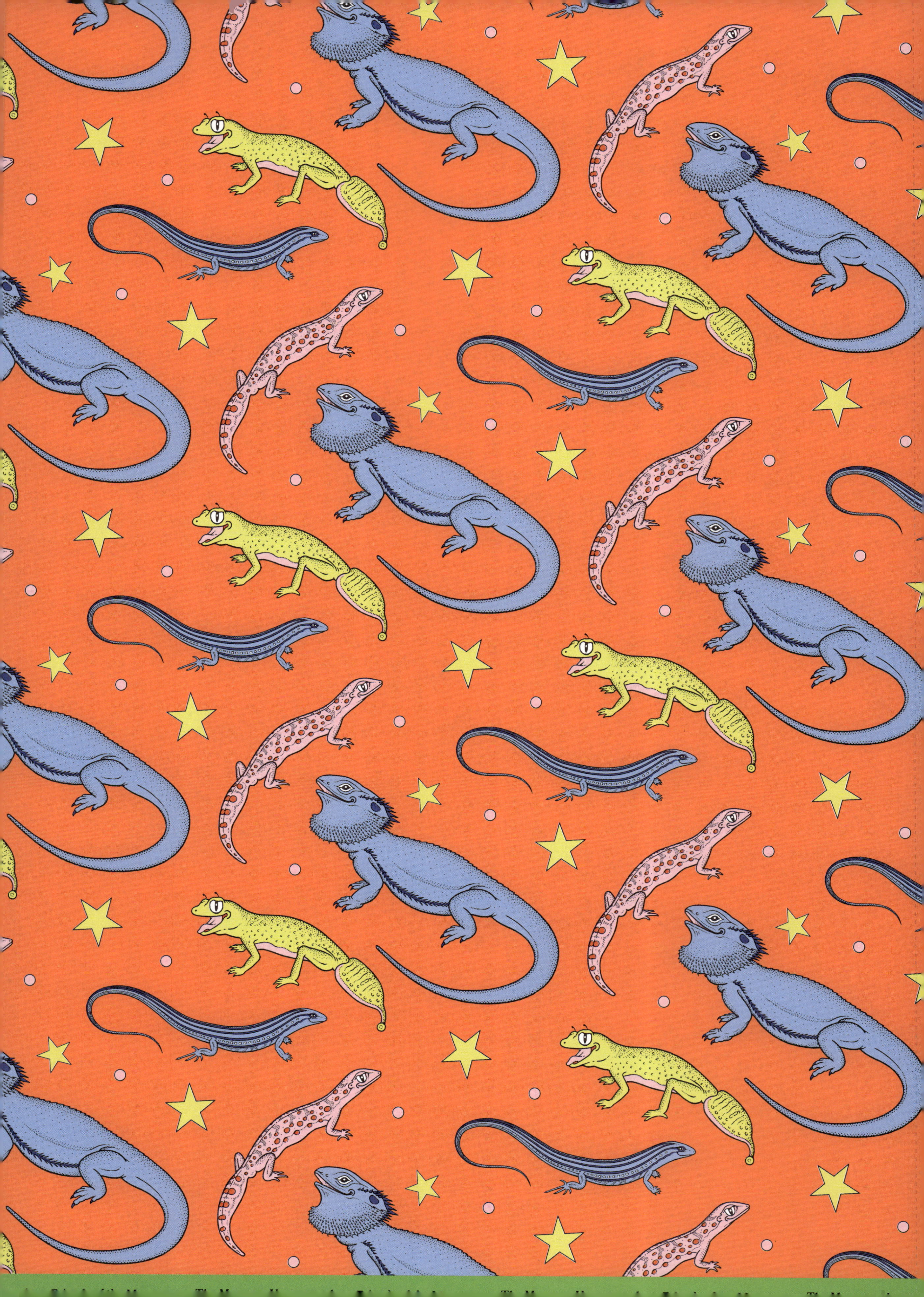

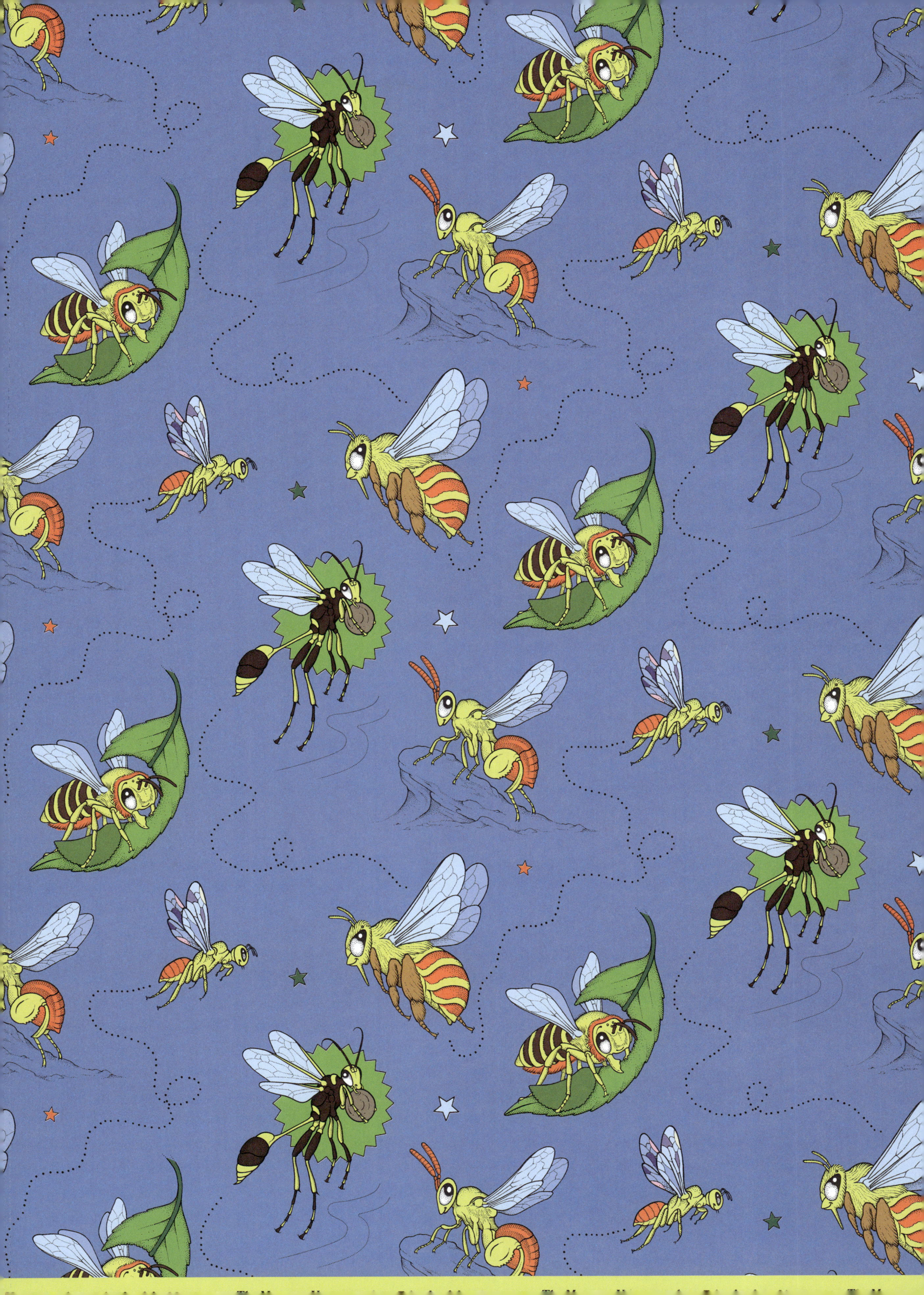

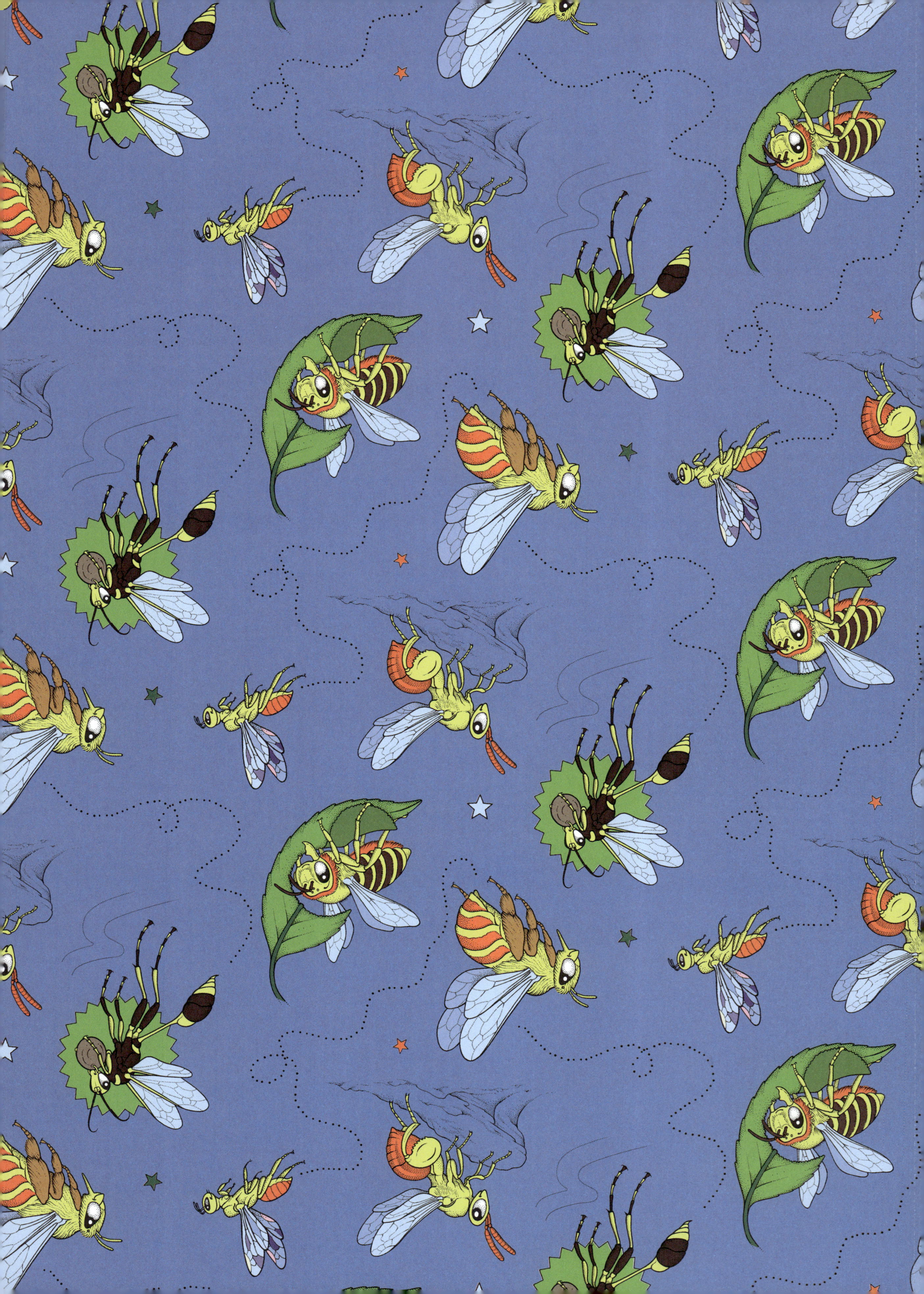

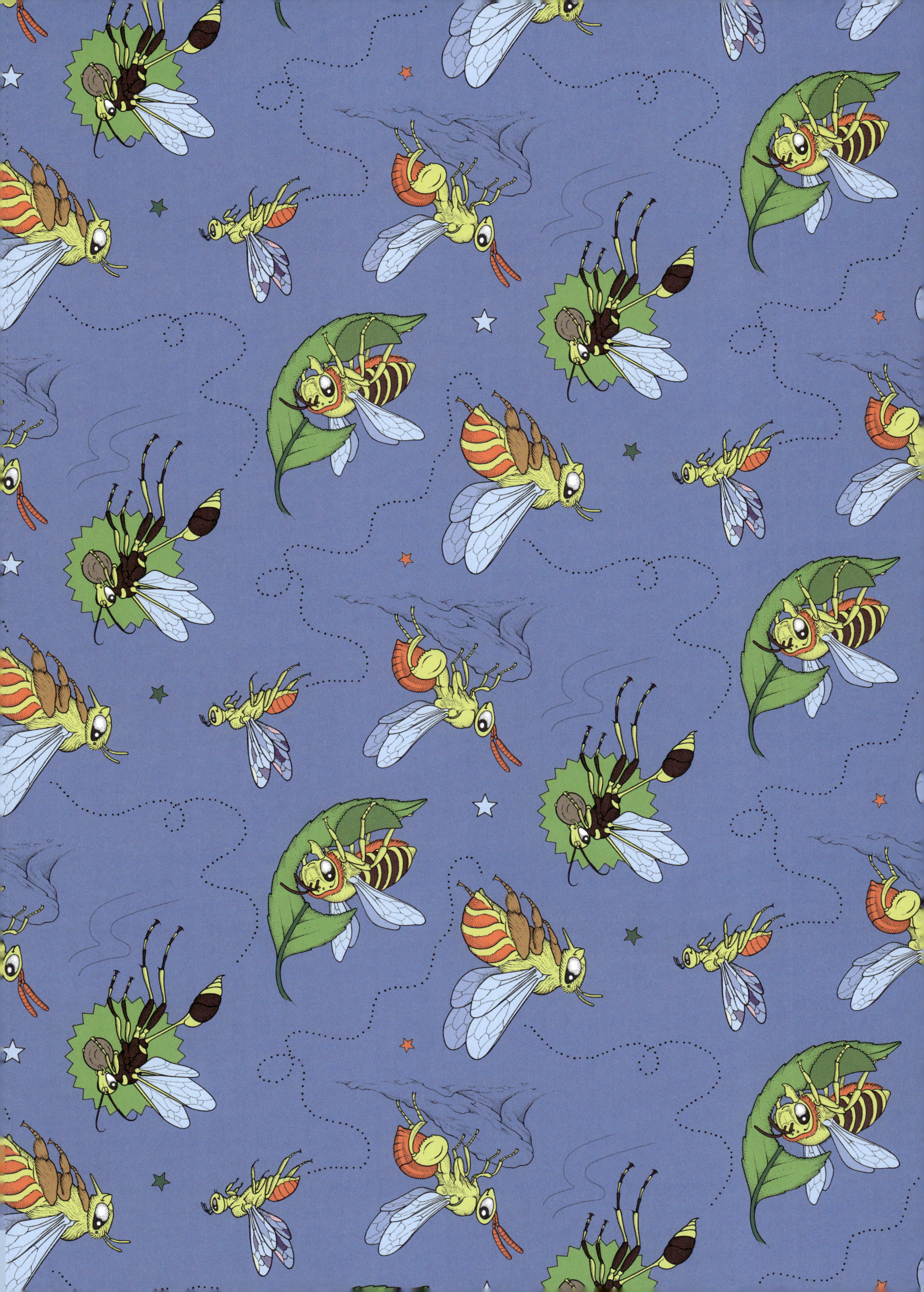

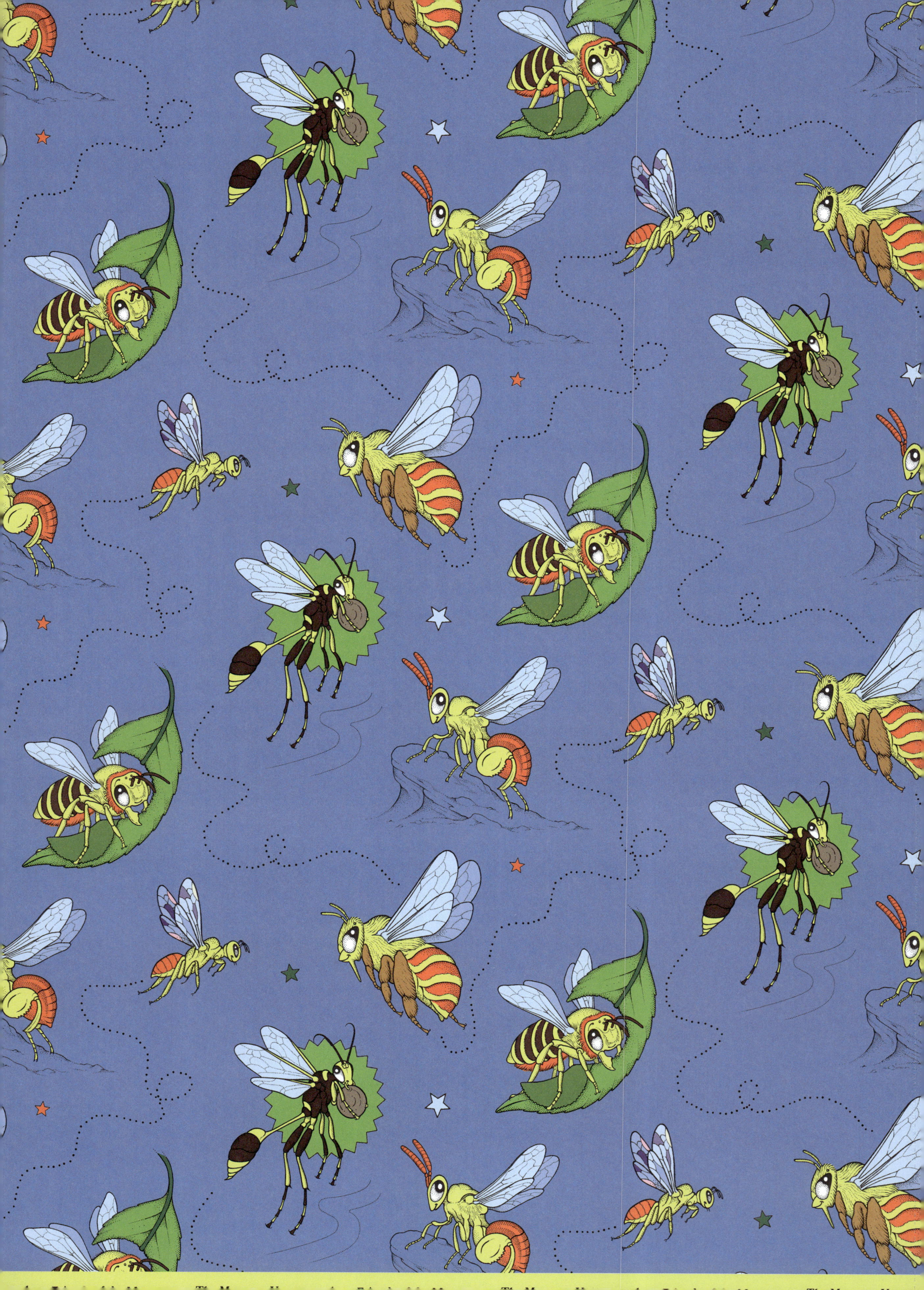

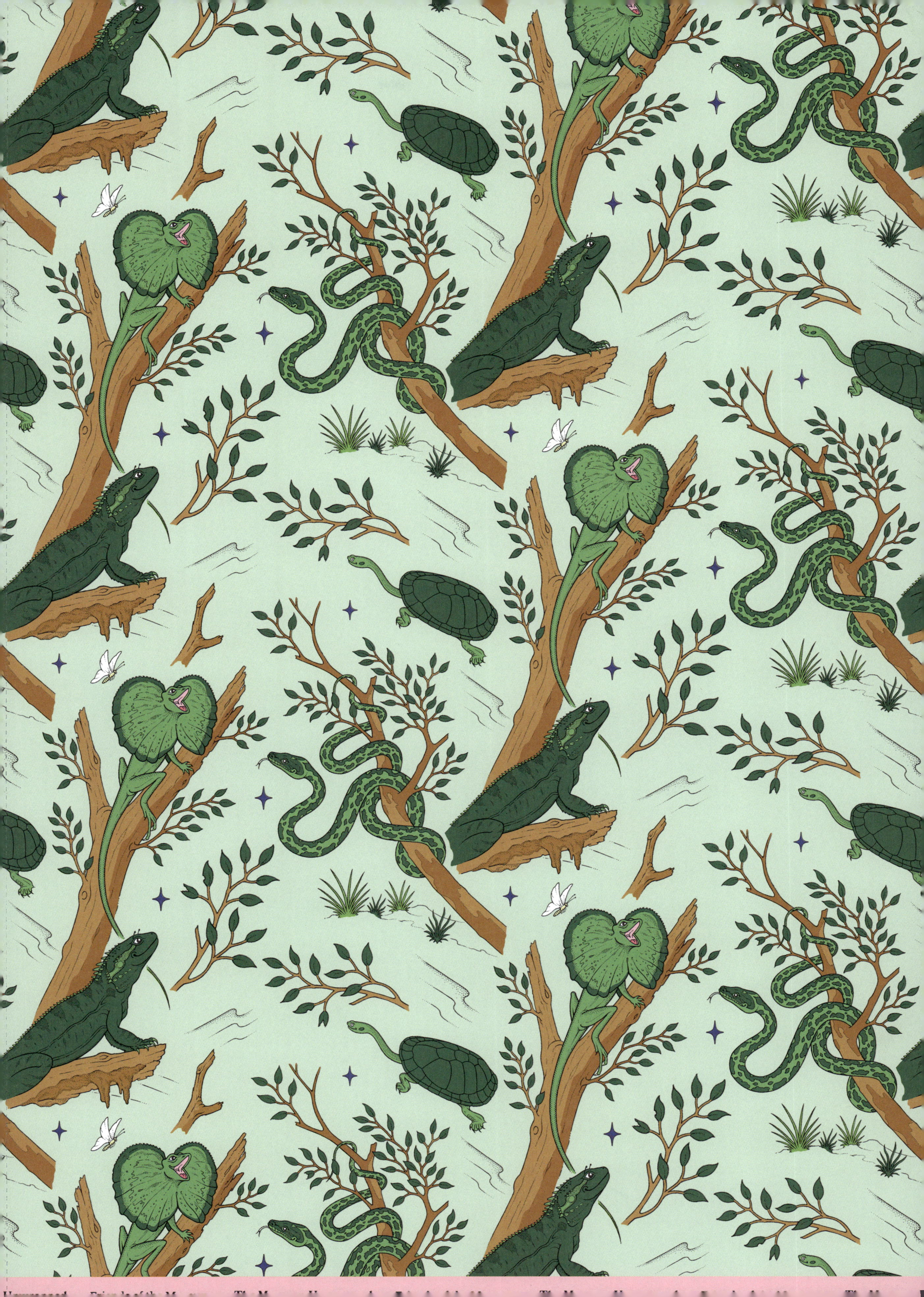

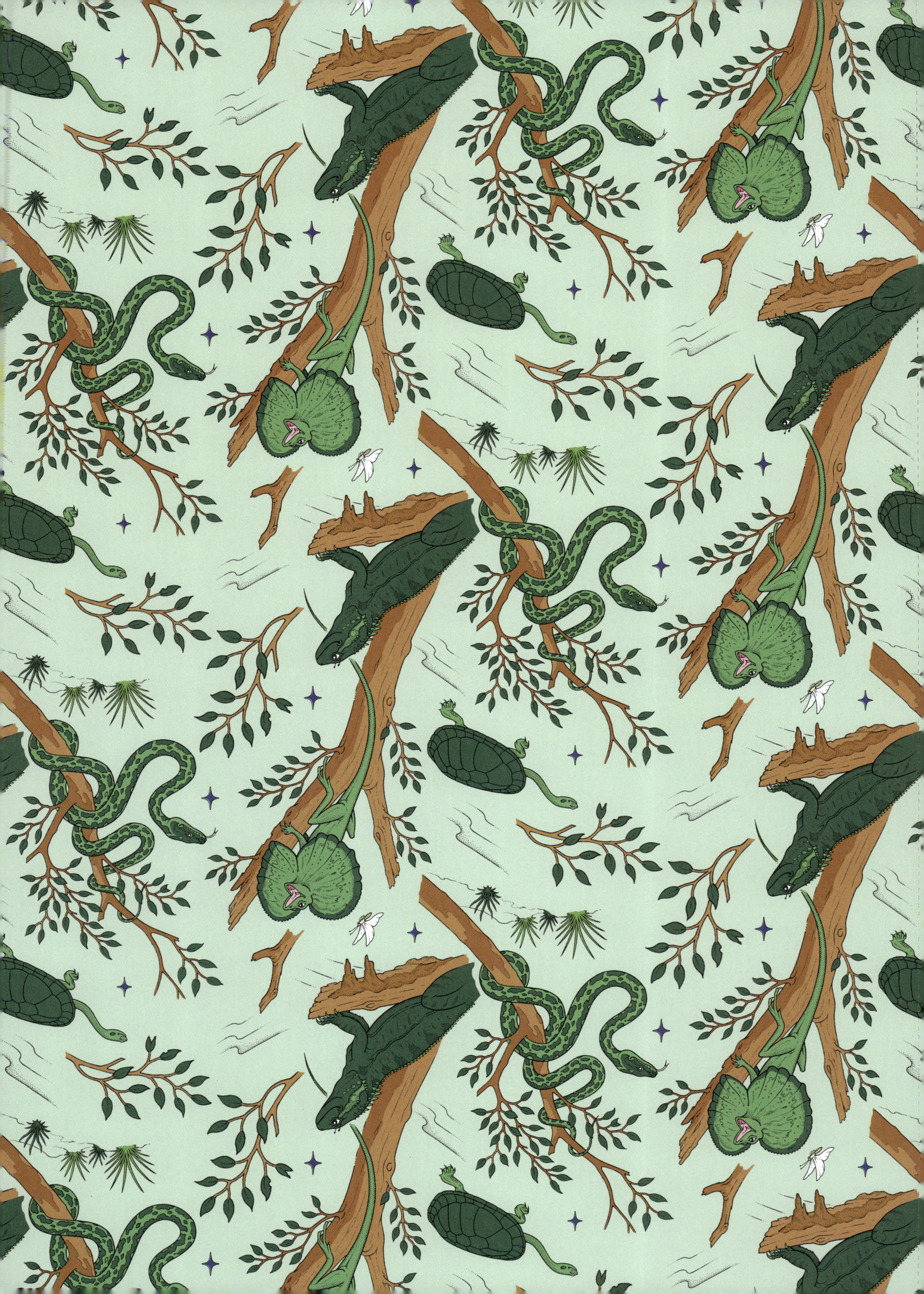

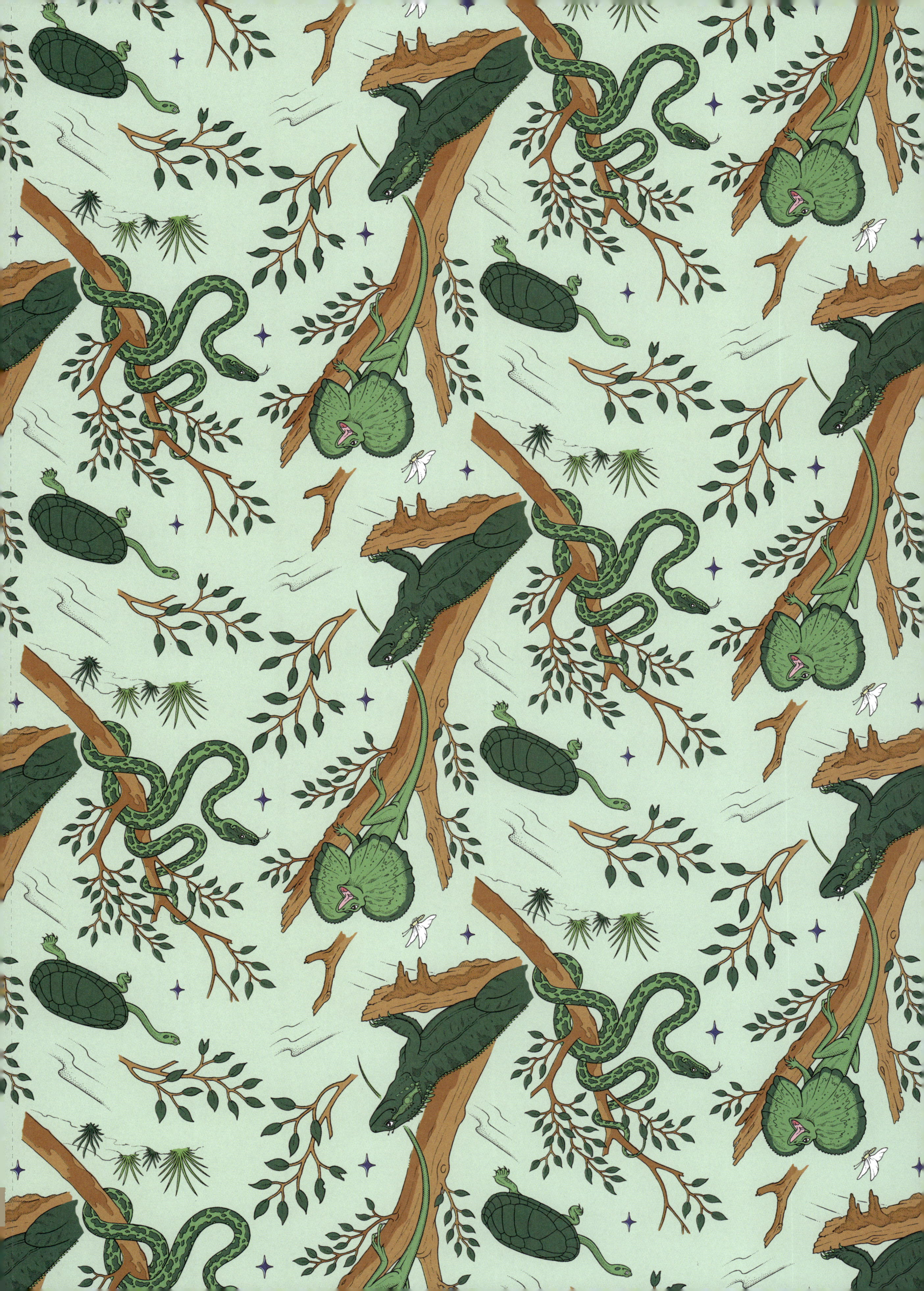

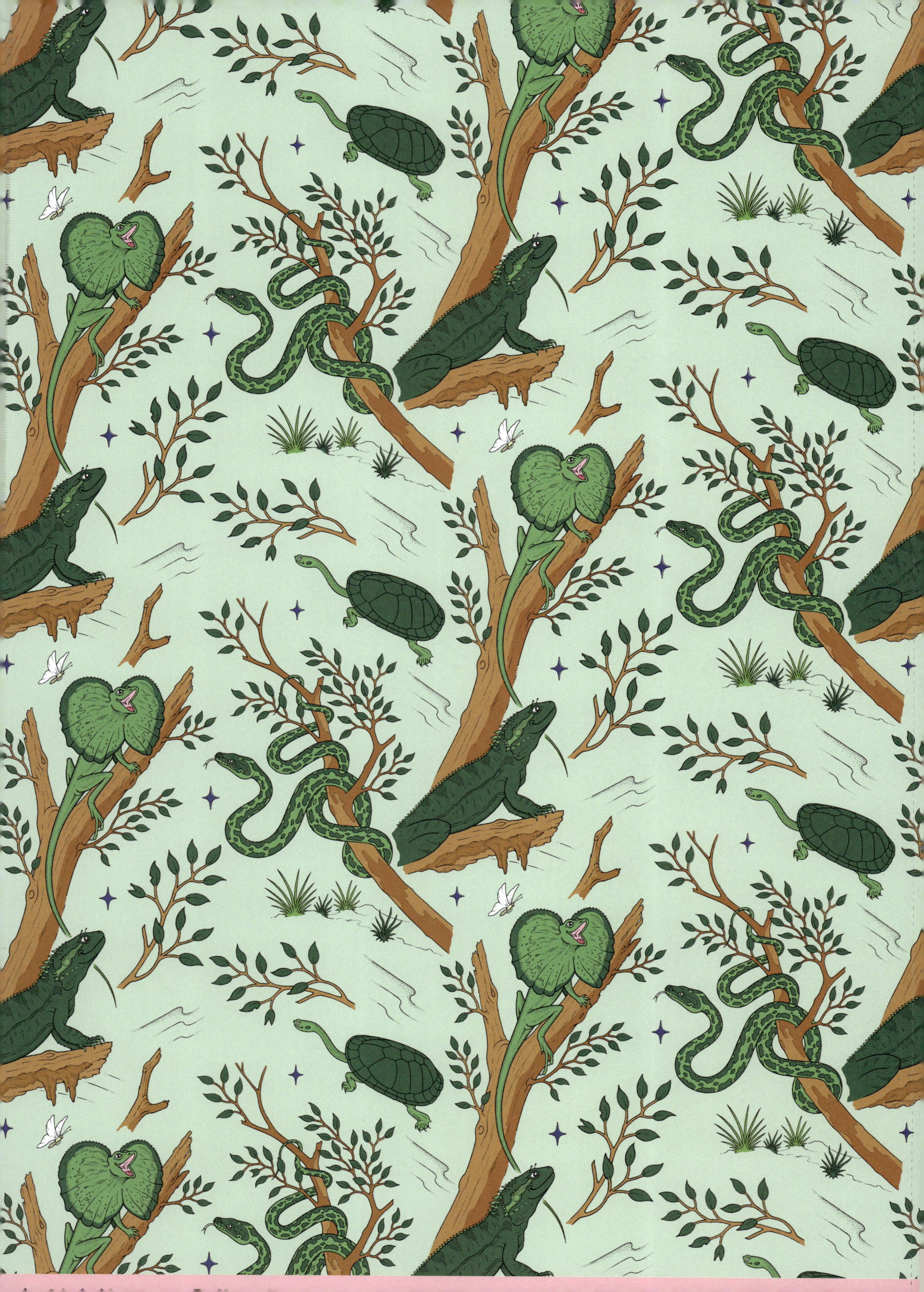

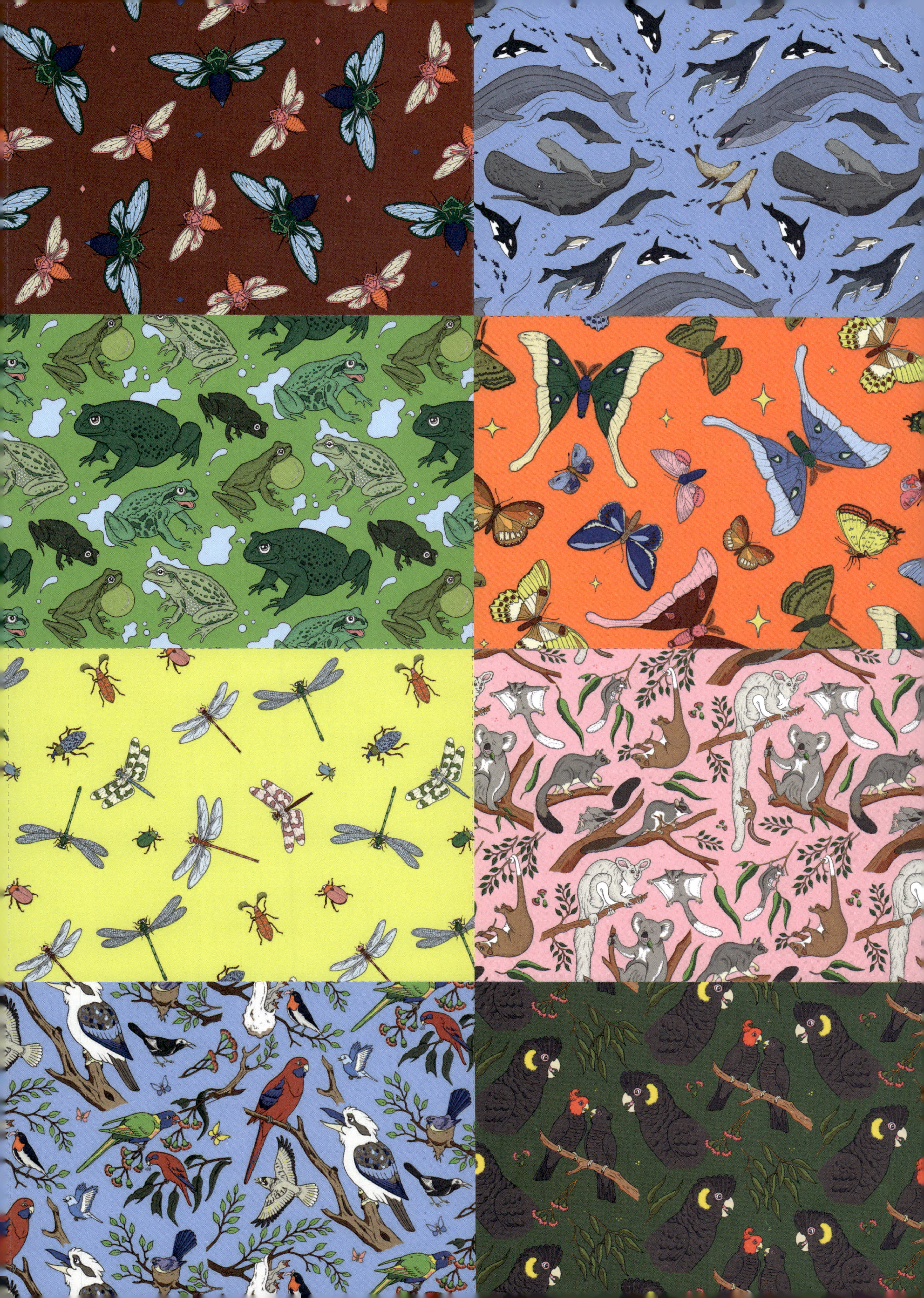

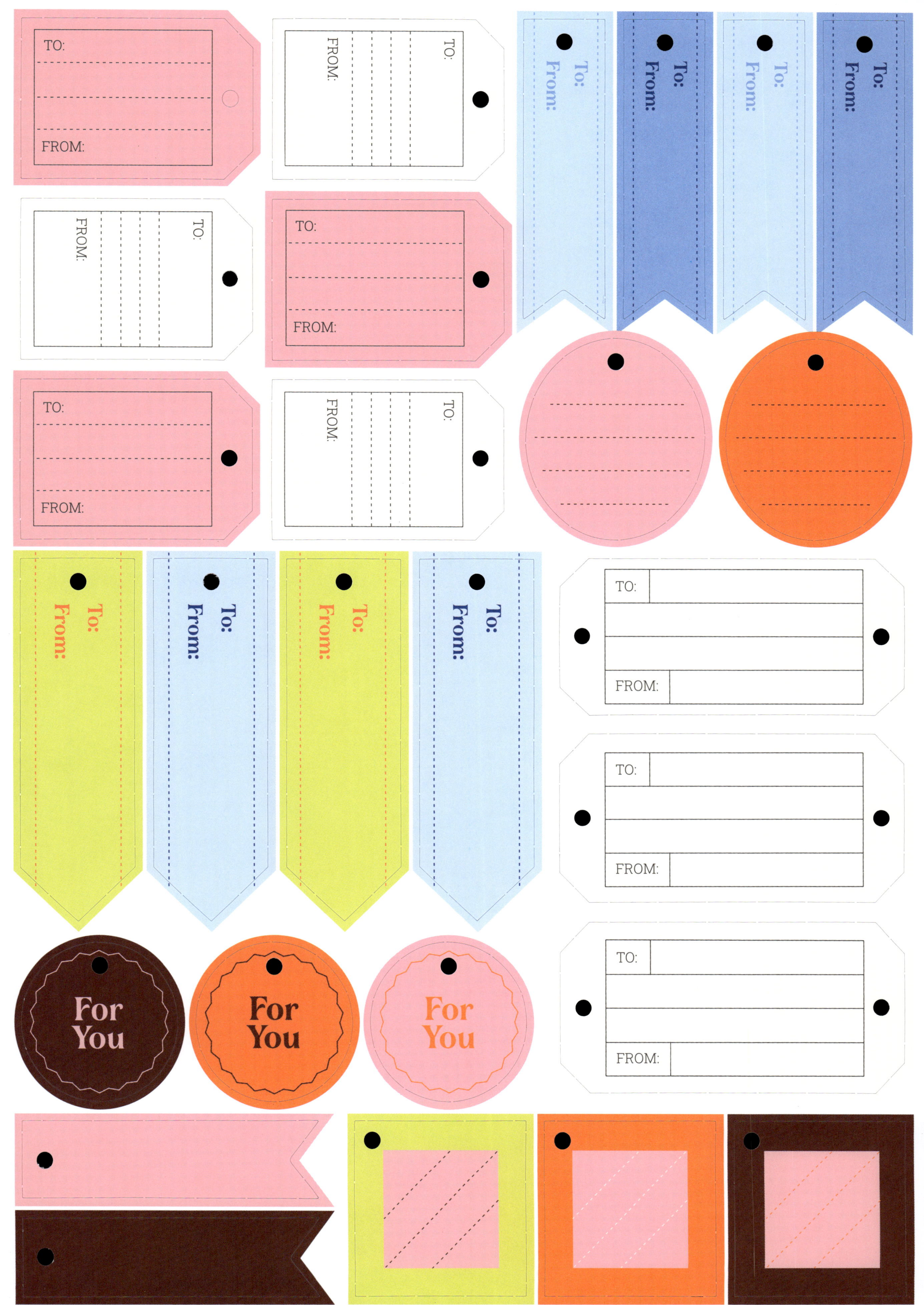
TO:
FROM:
TO:
FROM:
To:
From:
To:
From:
To:
From:
To:
From:
TO:
FROM:
TO:
FROM:
TO:
FROM:
TO:
FROM:
To:
From:
To:
From:
To:
From:
To:
From:
TO:
FROM:
TO:
FROM:
TO:
FROM:
For You
For You
For You

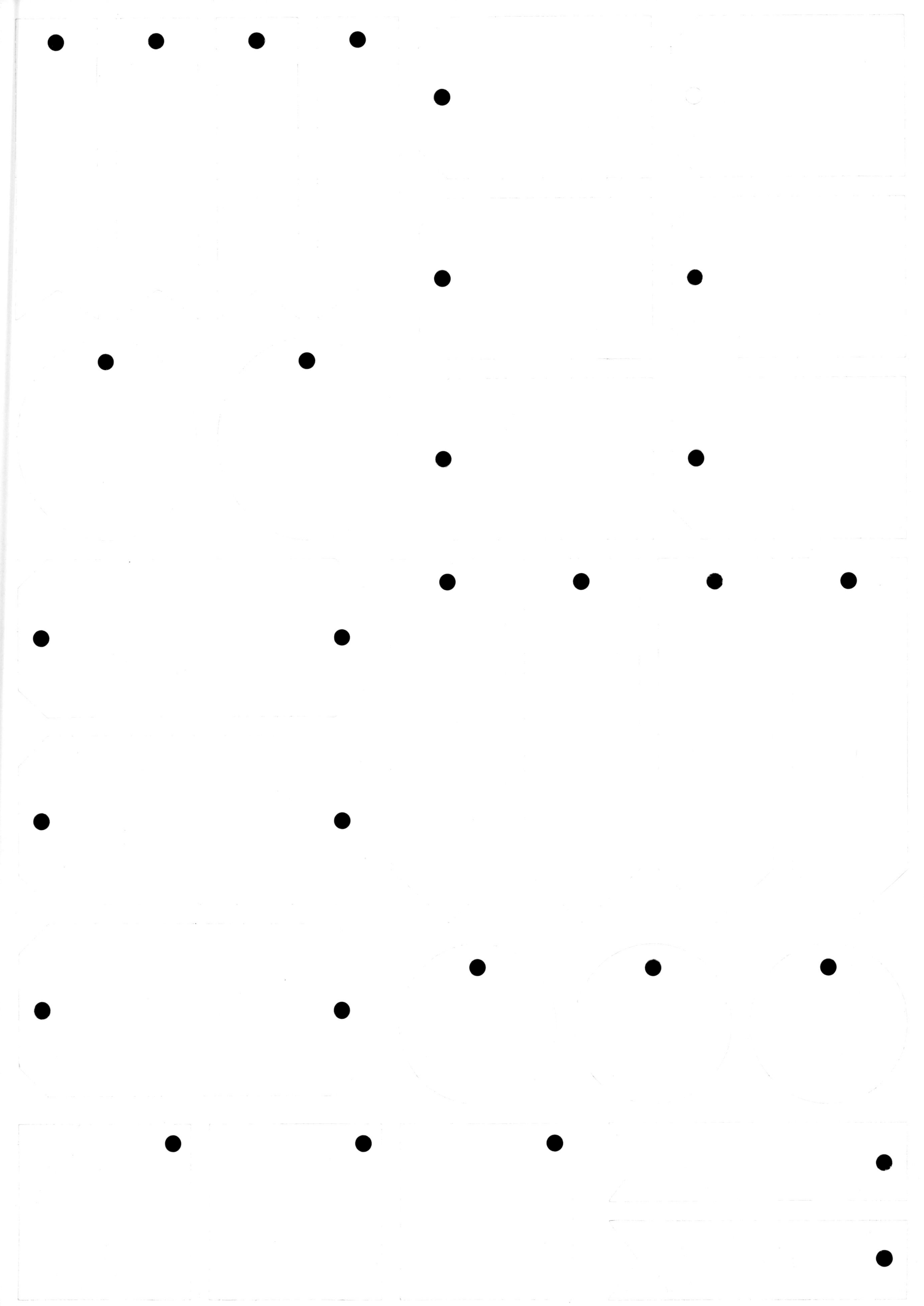